A TOXIC INCONVENIENCE

Red Tide and Blue-Green Algae on Florida's Coast

Nicholas G. Penniman IV

Barringer Publishing, Naples, Florida
www.barringerpublishing.com
Cover, graphics, layout design by Linda S. Leppert

Cover photography by Tom James, Pelican Media, LLC

ISBN: 978-1-7339837-7-8

Library of Congress Cataloging-in-Publication Data
A Toxic Inconvenience
Red Tide and Blue-Green Algae on Florida's Coast
Printed in U.S.A.

DEDICATION

This book is dedicated to my five grandchildren: Linda, Sarah, Nick, Henry, and Winnie.

I hope our generation and the next has the wisdom, the perspicacity and the political will to solve the problems set forth in this book and others that despoil our natural resources. If we do not, we will have failed and passed along to you, and your generation, an ailing planet perhaps beyond salvation.

PREFACE

This is a brief exposé, running only about one hundred eighty pages of text. I began to write it while looking out the window at the layer of dead fish covering Venetian and Moorings Bay, in Naples, Florida, in 2017. You could almost walk on it.

In trying to learn more about red tide beyond the daily news reports, I found here were no books written for the average reader that gave a history of red tide and some indication as to the state of research into human health issues, arising as a result of the growing outbreaks. In the process of doing research, I discovered that a cyanobacterium being released from Lake Okeechobee was causing a separate set of problems and that somehow it was all interrelated. So, I wrote the book in the hope that people would read it carefully and get angry enough to write or call their legislators to take action quickly.

This book does not do justice to the hundreds of thousands of pages, of great scientific research into the topic. I know that. As with all science, skepticism and questioning of assumptions and conclusions creates an ongoing dynamic of civil debate that is good and helpful and righteous. That is true in the case of red tide and blue-green algae as entirely separate natural phenomena. But as the subject of human health began to enter the picture, a new urgency infused the research efforts, an energy that continues today. Therefore, this book has to be considered a work in progress. While I have read over one hundred scientific papers that relate directly to southwest Florida, the full impact of harmful algae blooms on human health are not yet known. But there is a great deal of time and money now being spent looking into the subject. Thank goodness.

I am not a doctor, of either medicine or philosophy, but in order to provide the most accurate information possible, I have consulted physicians and academicians to confirm that what is written in this book adequately states the reality of human biological processes. The text is rigorously footnoted and I have to thank Dr. Larry Brand, Dr. Paul Cox, Dr. Dana Frank, M.D., Dr. Sandra Banack, Dr. Cindy Heil at Mote Marine and John Cassani for their thoughtful assistance. And thanks to my energetic wife who has put up with long periods of study, writing and revising, to Jeff Schlesinger, of Barringer Publishing, who has moved heaven and earth to get to get this book out on a timely basis, and to Tom James of Pelican Media LLC for his fantastic cover photo of algae blooming in the Caloosahatchee River at the Alva boat ramp.

TABLE OF CONTENTS

CHAPTER 1

Dorothy

◆——· ● ◆ ● ·——◆

Dorothy was born on the Mexican coast where the temperature of the beach sand, at the time, exceeded 82 degrees Fahrenheit.[1] She, along with her nestling siblings, entered the water at Rancho Nuevo and after swimming vigorously, for a day at about one knot per hour (within her yolk energy reserve), found herself exhausted but in the grasp of a horizontal venturi, a combination of two, counter-rotating current vortices that shoot small turtles out into the larger Florida Loop Current, where another series of surface currents and gyres distribute them throughout the Gulf.[2]

After about two years of floating around, Dorothy began to swim more vigorously, until she reached Florida's southwest coast where she was captured by a team of scientists from the Conservancy of Southwest Florida, Mote Marine Laboratories and the National Marine Fisheries Service.

The team had been studying sea turtle movements in response to water temperature changes and diet—mainly crabs—to determine management protocols to protect Kemps ridley turtles, the most endangered of the five species found in the Gulf of Mexico. Dorothy was a Kemps ridley.

After a few days in a holding tank, a transmitter was glued to her shell. Jeff Schmid, the Conservancy research scientist on the team, used an epoxy combination to cement the unit to her carapace. When asked how he thought Dorothy reacted to having to carry a research device around, Schmid replied: "She was probably none too happy about it. But after a while, I think it was acceptable. It wouldn't impair her ability to swim or forage."[3]

Once released, Dorothy went about seeking her favorite food in the waters of Pine Island Sound—the spider crab. She was able to cover the area quickly, swimming at one kilometer per hour, her long front flippers propelling her through the water, with her shorter, webbed rear flippers steering her. She needed to be alert as her prey was normally covered with algae and other forms of benthic camouflage, protected by spines on its carapace and a salivary secretion that acted like glue. But with her powerful beak, resembling that of a parrot, Dorothy was able to crack the outer shell and feast upon the meat of spider crabs in the sound. Their size and relatively soft shell made them ideal prey, although she would occasionally settle for a few delectable clams or mussels.

Then, for some unknown reason, Dorothy decided to move from the sound out into the open waters of the Gulf of Mexico.

Sea turtle research indicates that as Kemp's ridleys grow older, they tend to cover larger areas. Turtles with a relatively small carapace, of twenty-five to thirty-five centimeters, tended to be very active in and out of the passes along Pine Island Sound but stayed generally in the nearshore area. Dorothy, with a carapace of forty-eight centimeters, was classified as a sub-adult capable of ranging widely into deeper water. Her diet there would change. She would be ingesting urochordates or tunicates—sea squirts and sea worms. Normally found attached to the underside of docks, piers and boats, these small creatures have a semi-hard, outer covering which looks like a tunic, thus giving them their name, but will affix to any hard bottom surface. Closely related to vertebrates, one branch of tunicates are pelagic wanderers and become the source of the phosphorescent light, sometimes seen in boat wakes at night. And, as Dorothy's diet changed, the risk increased that she would ingest human detritus: fishing line, rope, string or cigarette filters that might resemble her prey.

Dorothy's move to the Gulf remained a mystery to Jeff Schmid. Most creatures, including early humans, adopt what is called "optimal foraging strategy" which, in its simplest form, is a decision to obtain the highest energy input (food source) for the lowest energy expenditure (effort to acquire the food). For Dorothy to move away from the smorgasbord available in Pine Island Sound, other factors had to be at work.

One possibility, according to Schmid, is that, as a

sub-adult, she simply preferred the offshore environment to the sound. "Another possible explanation was that there was a brief spike in the red tide counts in the Sound several days before Dorothy departed and perhaps this was the stimulus for her to move out."[4] But her decision to move was unfortunate, for Dorothy unknowingly swam into a much larger and potent outbreak of red tide.

Whatever the reason, it did not serve Dorothy well. As later measured by Mote Marine Laboratory, in a chlorophyll overlay reconstruction of the offshore outbreak, she found herself in the middle of an environmental disaster, about five kilometers west of Sanibel Island. She was ingesting bottom-dwelling tunicates laced with red tide toxins while at the same time swimming through the algae-loaded soup. Telemetry data showed that she then moved ten kilometers southeast along the coast to a location where she stayed for a week, and then swam out further west. By October 29, 2011, Dorothy's radio signal was consistent and uninterrupted, meaning she had surfaced and was no longer moving.[5] Then abruptly, her signal ceased.

When asked about the incident, Schmid expressed confusion as to why Dorothy would stay in the middle of a red tide concentration. "That's the 'million dollar' question. Most of the other ones we have tracked, when they sense the algae—they avoid it. They move away. I don't know what happened here."[6]

Red tide

While Dorothy's ancestors are ancient; red tide is as well. But, in just the past fifty years, red tide has increased in coverage, frequency and duration. Red tide consists of dinoflagellates as a naturally occurring part of the Gulf of Mexico ecosystem. Starting offshore in deeper water, on the West Florida Shelf, concentrations of the algae periodically move toward the land. Why—no one knows for certain. It may be related to seasonal changes in the Florida Loop Current and its gyres. It may be wind driven.

One theory suggests that red tide initiation and growth is accelerated by warming water, which is why the phenomenon originates in the fall and not year-round (although it is becoming more prevalent off coastal southwest Florida, during the tourist season), but scientific consensus points to a massive increase in the background levels, until certain known stimuli awaken it, nourish it, and move it into coastal waters where nutrients exist in abundance.

Most red tide outbreaks throughout the world are observed in nearshore areas. By inference, it might be reasonable to assume that coastal runoff from southwest Florida urban and exurban development (leaking septic tanks) and agriculture (particularly urea nitrogen and phosphorous) acts as an accelerator—like a supercharger on an internal combustion engine. This is the conclusion in a University of Miami study where the authors squarely place blame for higher concentrations of *Karenia brevis* on coastal runoff, high in land-based nutrients.[7]

On the other hand, one of the leading research institutions into the causes and effects of the phenomenon, Mote Marine Laboratories, is still struggling to arrive at a scientifically plausible explanation as to causality.

These two differing opinions, from respected scientific institutions, are an example of one of the main themes of this book: the ongoing debate between respected scientists as to the causes of red tide outbreaks, blooms and termination. Science is inductive and empirical, based upon observation and measurement, living within the realm of skepticism and uncertainty, until evidence gradually builds toward an inescapable conclusion—an objective truth that is discoverable through the rigorous scientific process. This will be examined, over time, framed as a debate and possibly influenced by special interests, in Florida, intent upon preserving the *status quo.*

The second theme, using studies of salt-water red tide and fresh-water cyanobacteria, is the tendency of regulatory agencies to deal with effects, not causes. There are differences between coincidence, correlation and causality. It is when the hard fact of unquestioned, verified causality has been scientifically settled that policy must enter the picture.

This is the point where the curtain on "analysis paralysis" is pulled back and decisions are thrust upon the wizards of the political realm. The uncertainty of the scientific process has allowed policy makers to argue that the science is not settled, but as we shall see, the day of reckoning may be fast approaching because of the impacts on Florida's economy and even more importantly, on human health.

This is the third theme: impacts upon human health. The respiratory effects of red tide on humans have been studied since the 1940s, and the death toll on aquatic life has been observed and reported for hundreds of years. This book will examine what we know about red tide and how we came to know it. But in the last decade, another form of algae, fresh-water cyanobacteria, has come to plague the southwest coast of Florida.

After capturing Guam from the Japanese during World War II, a naval neurologist noticed a cluster of neurodegenerative illnesses similar to amyotrophic lateral sclerosis (ALS), among the Chamorro people on the island. Subsequent research, led by ethnobotanist Paul Cox and Dartmouth physician Elijah Stommel, identified similar disease clusters proximate to bodies of fresh water in the northeastern United States. Research done by Cox is convincing and, if finally verified, the source of the problem is in pulses of toxic water from Lake Okeechobee that are released at the wrong time of year, pouring down the Caloosahatchee River into Charlotte Harbor. The push back against Cox's evidence has been forceful, the main argument being that studies to date have demonstrated correlation but failed to prove causality.

As with all science, the process of peer review will ultimately lead to the best outcome, and this book will chronicle the appearance of blue-green algae in southwest

Florida estuaries, during the mid-1990s, when it begins to have effects upon coastal communities and caused public health authorities to realize that it posed the possibility of long-term human health impacts greater than red tide. However, if Cox and Stommel are right, the problem is in our backyard.

The next two chapters will cover three centuries of discovery history and explain how knowledge unfolded. Later chapters will chronicle how the scientific community, through the exacting process of banging heads in peer reviewed articles and presentations, came to close the circle on the problem.

It will cover what we *know* today about the life cycle of red tide blooms, from science over the past three decades. It will also chronicle how government and regulatory authorities dealt with the ever-expanding base of knowledge. In some instances, it was simply a matter of complacency. In others, how willful ignorance or artfully designed alternative strategies were developed to divert the public's attention from the real issues to less relevant ones, in order to protect special interests.

What follows is a tale, of how the unwillingness to admit the obvious, has created a potential perfect storm for the people and the environment of the Sunshine State.

The significance of Dorothy

Why is the story of Dorothy important? It unfolds a narrative that could only be told through careful observation, by trained scientists attempting to achieve a better understanding of how the natural world works or, in the case of Dorothy, how sometimes the rules of nature are violated—leading to a tragic outcome.

Sea turtles are an "indicator species." Appearing for the first time around 150 million years ago, while dinosaurs went slowly extinct during the Cretaceous era, sea turtles survived and eventually thrived. The study of sea turtles provides a robust source of information as to how we manage coastal and aquatic resources, in mute testament to human stewardship, of the domain of these appealing creatures. If we manage well, with our superb technology, backed by a broad level of understanding and public support, we will continue to thrive as a nation and as a state.

To understand *how* we know all we do, and what might be done about it, we need to turn back the clock to the beginning of the 16th century, during the era of Spanish exploration, of the Gulf of Mexico, and their discoveries of what might have been red tide.

CHAPTER 2

Early History

◆——·•◆•·——◆

It was first observed in the 16th century by Alvar Núñez Cabeza de Vaca, a survivor of the ill-fated Panfilo de Narvaez expedition, in 1528, seeking to explore and colonize the Gulf of Mexico coastline, between Florida and the Rio Grande River. Hurricanes and hostile natives wrought havoc on the expedition, but de Vaca and three others survived, reaching Mexico City in 1537 and Spain in 1538, to author an extraordinary ethnography—the first ever documentation of native American tribal culture and traditions. In his memoirs, de Vaca mentions fish kills but in an ambiguous way: "[the natives] judge of the seasons by the ripening of the fruits, by the time the fish die ..." [8]

A more authoritative text came a century later from Fray Diego Lopez de Collugudo. In 1648, he described a fish kill near the Yucatan peninsula of Mexico: "A short time later ... for several days, especially in the evenings when the wind blows from the sea, came a foul odor that at times could barely be tolerated, as it penetrated all parts.

11

No one knew the cause of the odor until a ship from Spain encountered a mountain of dead fish near the coast. Dead fish were heaped on shore, and this is where the foul odor emanated." [9]

The problem with this description is there is no mention of time of year. Fish kills occur for different reasons—prolonged cold weather being one, so the assumption that red tide is the culprit is a stretch at best without further context.

The Spanish reports then died off, because there was little interest in Florida during the 17th and first half of the 18th centuries. The territory was ill-defined when Florida was ceded to England, after the French and Indian War. Twenty years later, the Treaty of Paris transferred Florida, from British control back to Spanish control, until 1821, when the newly formed United States took control after the Adams—Onis Treaty defined the boundaries of the Louisiana Purchase. In 1845, with the current boundary lines in effect, Florida was admitted to the Union as its 27th state.

During this period, covering almost two hundred years, Florida was regarded as an afterthought, by the prevailing world powers. The Spanish found none of the riches they expected, and the British used the state's east coast for military purposes. There was little population growth, since much of the state was still occupied and controlled by native tribes, until the Second Seminole War ended in 1842.

A few isolated reports of fish kills, in the Gulf, appeared

in local newspapers, until 1875, when a large outbreak occurred along the Gulf Coast, causing significant human respiratory distress, i.e. coughing and a gaseous odor (probably from dead fish) were reported. This prompted one Spanish investigator, Núñez Ortega, to opine that marine volcanic eruptions off Veracruz, Mexico, were poisoning the Gulf waters and creating the outbreak.[10]

Science enters the picture

Ernest Ingersoll, while at Harvard, was a zoology student studying under the eminent Louis Agassiz. Upon his mentor's death in 1873, Ingersoll joined the staff of New York's *Herald Tribune,* where he honed his writing skills but eventually found the work unsatisfying. He traveled to Colorado and found that adventure, animated by intellectual curiosity and attention to detail, made for an ideal combination, allowing him to explore the world and publish his observations in the best-selling periodicals of the day like *Harper's Weekly* and *Scribner's.*

Joining the U. S. Fish Commission in 1881, Ingersoll was sent to southwest Florida, to investigate a large outbreak of marine life devastation, where he created the first comprehensive written record of damage to the entire ecosystem. His monographs, written for the Commission on Shellfishing Practices, were superb ethnographies combining science, observation, history, interviews, theoretical knowledge and personal anecdotes. This wide range of journalistic components pervades his 1881 report on a fish kill in southwest Florida "... to inquire into the so-called "poisoned water" which was supposed to have caused the remarkable mortality among the sea-fishes that occurred in the autumn of 1880."[11]

Relying upon the memories of some of south Florida's oldest residents, Ingersoll captured the 1844 fish kill and a series of events beginning in 1854 and continuing sporadically each fall, until 1878, that devastated the fishing industry of south Florida. The winter "wet season," of 1878-1879, saw extraordinarily heavy amounts of rainfall, with both the Manatee and Caloosahatchee Rivers overflowing their banks and inundating the coastal estuaries with fresh water loaded with tannins. Locals, fishing captains and processors, all saw this as the cause of the die-off, but Ingersoll was not convinced.

Based on his observations, freshwater discharges might cause deaths in isolated spots, but not generally and not throughout the water column.

"In regard to some of the manifestations of this deadly influence in the sea during 1878, Mr. John Brady, Jr., an intelligent captain, told me that the time of year was January, and that the "poisoned water", to which universal belief credits the death of the fishes, could easily be distinguished from the clear blue of the pure surrounding element. This discolored water appeared in long patches, or "streaks", sometimes 100 yards wide, drifting lengthways with the flow of the tide."[12]

The destruction was further amplified by the keeper of the Egmont Key lighthouse, Charles Moore, who wrote that sponges, crabs (particularly horseshoe crabs), oysters and clams were washing up on the beaches. He noted that oysters and clams being dredged from Tampa Bay had become weak and tasteless, with a "repulsive green hue at their edges." [13]

"It was the death of sponges, conchs, sea-anemones, crawling horseshoe crabs, of toad-fish cow-fish, skates, and the like which keep close to the bottom that first apprised the fishermen of the presence of the dreaded and mysterious enemy. Next came the carcasses of red fish, groupers, pompanos, and other deep swimmers, and last of all a few mullets and sharks. Fresh water would not affect this." [14]

Ingersoll then took a leap of faith. While admitting he had not taken samples of the water to analyze chemical content, he concluded that "poison" springs beneath the West Florida Shelf, created by the eruption of volcanic gas stretching from Tampa Bay to the Dry Tortugas, was the only likely culprit with the capacity to wreak such damage. He had anecdotal evidence of an earthquake around Christmas of 1877, and hypothecated that the shock waves may have opened vents in the limestone, releasing toxic fumes made soluble by the springs, that did the damage to aquatic organisms up and down the entire water column.

The fish kill, of 1878 to 1880, was remarkable for its broad geographic coverage and duration. In an 1882 letter written to Professor John Bair, Commissioner of Fish and Fisheries in Washington, D.C., a Mr. M. A. Moore opined that creatures of the benthic habitat were more affected than the mobile species, pointing to volcanic action as the likely cause of destruction. Another series of letters to Bair, from fishermen based in the Dry Tortugas, noted that in Florida Bay, during the fall in 1878, the water had a blackish, cypress look. Data indicates that in 1880, Florida vessels landed 1.5 million pounds of red snapper—one-third of the normal catch reported in Florida ports ten years later. [15]

The final blow came on the subject of human health. During that same month of November 1880, a letter came to Spencer Baird, Secretary of the Smithsonian Institution from a Mrs. Hoy of Manatee County who remarked that:

"In regard to oysters I have had a rather rough experience and can say with certainty that they are poisonous. A few days after the fish began dying I had a quart of fine oysters for dinner . . . my daughter and I ate heartily of them . . . a visitor on that day . . . did not like oysters and ate none . . . I began to feel weak, and a mist came before my eyes . . . was so blind . . . my daughter similarly affected and unable to walk . . . the visitor—nor my cook were affected, which makes me know it was the oysters. The sickness and loss of vision gradually left us after drinking a cup of strong coffee." [16]

This report was the first extensively documented instance of the effects of red tide on human health posed by red tide, carefully documented from a woman with an obviously vigorous appetite for oysters.

Ingersoll's report, compelling and fulsome, did stir some further inquiry. The fishing industry along Florida's southwest coast, one of the state's economic engines at the time, had been devastated. Commercial fishing captains, processors and all the people employed by the industry suffered economic hardship, for nearly two years, prompting some desultory reports by the federal government and the United States Commission of Fish and Fisheries (commonly known as the U. S. Fish Commission), created in 1871, to respond to the crisis. The Commission had been formed to investigate the reasons for declining fish population in coastal waters, and to recommend measures to bring the population back. The die-off from 1878 and 1880-1881 were the first real crises it faced, but the response was basically to study and chronicle the incidents . . . a response that would be repeated time and time again by federal and state authorities.

The Commission's report took almost five years to complete. In the meantime, blooms continued to occur. In 1882, a report appeared in the *Sunland Tribune* with descriptive substance:

"We learn from Captain William Jackson, of the steamer

Lizzie Henderson, that on a trip from Cedar Key, Tuesday, he encountered a "streak" of poisoned water, covered with all varieties of dead fish, of more than a mile in extent, off Indian Pass, between Clearwater and Egmont Light. The captain says that a very offensive smell arose from it, and that a good many bottom fish, such as eels, were floating on the surface." [17] The most important word is "streak," which will appear repeatedly in a number of future scientific reports on red tide. The streaks amounted to long, thin tendrils of discolored water indicating movement of the red tide bloom up and down the Florida coast, an important element in understanding the life cycle of red tide outbreaks.

That same year produced a number of reports of fish kills up and down the Florida coast. In an exchange of letters, published by the U. S. National Museum, two scientists speculated that the mortality of fish was caused by a volcanic eruption.[18] A later report, in an 1885 article, reported that fish had been killed in an October event of "reddish-colored" water moving from Charlotte Harbor to Egmont Key, but was brief and only slightly descriptive.[19]

In 1885, when finally an extensive report was made public by the Commission, it gave reasons for the rapidly declining fish population in the Gulf of Mexico as "...probably partly overfishing in particular localities, partly the numerous pestilences and mortalities by which so many are exterminated." It then dismissed all possible causes but one, albeit unlikely. "No satisfactory theory has been presented for this mortality, although an intelligent writer suggests that is due to the influx of the cold water found near the sea bottom at great depth . . . ."[20]

In the final analysis, Ingersoll proposed no solutions. His volcanic gas theory was not accepted by the conservative Commission, but he did create a record that began a long process of documenting nature's devastation of one of America's great resources. Nothing was done, until 1916, when another massive outbreak occurred.

1916

Harden Taylor was a career employee of the U. S. Bureau of Fisheries. He was much published and would be known for his pioneering work, in the use of salt to preserve freshly caught fish. The Bureau was originally the U. S. Fish Commission that employed Ernest Ingersoll but had been moved, in 1903, into the Department of Commerce, reflecting a growing awareness of the economic importance of the industry.

In 1916, Taylor was dispatched to southwest Florida to report back on a massive fish-kill. "Repeatedly in the past seven years reports have come from the west coast of Florida on 'poison water' which killed fish in large numbers, and also, according to some reports, other animals, notably sponges."[21] This quote, from his report published by the Bureau in 1917, was the second attempt to scientifically analyze and document fish deaths along the Florida coast.

George Skermer was deputy collector of customs at Boca Grande, and a capable observer. In corresponding with Taylor, still in Washington preparing to leave for southwest Florida, he described the "poison water" as having covered an area from Sarasota to Naples, as far offshore as twenty miles, and noted that fish were dying, as they passed through dark-colored "streaks." In his response, Taylor speculated that the phytoplankton *Peridinium* might be the problem—as it would in 2016, with a disastrous release from Lake Okeechobee down the Caloosahatchee River. Skermer was dismissive of the idea, but Taylor was convinced and would later try to prove it out in his field work.

Part of Taylor's problem was that he was hampered by a lack of prior analysis, with little available beyond Ingersoll's studies and a few anecdotal and somewhat confused reports of kills, in areas containing discolored water. A student of history, he then began to rely more heavily upon observations from around the world, especially those coming from lines of latitude parallel to southwest Florida, where Taylor soon made his way.

Once he got there, his narrative powers were in full display as recorded in his description of the October 1916 fish kill at Boca Grande Pass:

"Fishes of a great number of species were noted dead and dying; the air was charged with a suffocating gas, which not only occasioned sever discomfort to man and other air-breathing animals, but irritated the air passages, producing the symptoms of colds. This gas, while exceedingly irritating, had not odor. The fishing smacks which are equipped with "wells" or openings through to the water in which fish are kept report that the whole catch dies while the smacks were enroute to port; the normal color of the water had given way to water of a different color, variously described as "black streaky," "amber," "olive," and "red;" the white paint of certain houses near the water was temporarily blackened, apparently by gases from the enormous number of dying fish . . . The abnormal conditions seemed to be moving southward." [22]

The bloom was still going strong in November. Taylor described his walks along the beach:

"On the dark nights of that week, the phosphorescence of the decaying fishes made the beach visible for long distance, and the sand was so charged with phosphorescent bacteria that one's tracks persisted for some seconds. Familiar fishes were identified by their own light. The odor was almost intolerable; people dwelling on the islands hauled away wagonloads and buried them in their orchards for fertilizer." [23]

By mid-November, a cold front came roaring through Fort Myers, dropping the Gulf temperature about 4° Celsius, but the fish kill continued unabated. While interviewing fishermen, Taylor learned that during the peak period of mortality, the water turned from olive-colored to a darker brown or amber, appearing in streaks or elongated strips on the surface.

One fisherman relayed a story about a large mullet that died within two minutes of passing through discolored water. After necropsy of dozens of fish species and exhaustive interviews, and a study of similar disasters around the world, Taylor was convinced that a seismic event must have triggered the bloom so he turned to another friend, Professor J. B. Woodworth, of the Harvard seismographic station, for advice. Woodworth had established, in 1908, one of the most highly instrumented facilities for data collection in the world and was widely regarded as the foremost expert in his field, and Taylor had read about massive fish kills, after earthquakes in the Sumesari River in India. Woodworth was doubtful that this was the cause of the problem, because the U. S. Weather Bureau had no record of seismic activity in the Gulf of Mexico in 1916 but Taylor remained stubbornly obdurate, and, in his report, he wrote:

"The causes suggested are (1) water from the Everglades charged with tannin and decomposition of palmettos and mangroves; (2) extraordinary presence of Peridinium known to have occasioned the death of fishes in other parts of the world; (3) a disease, fungoid, parasitic or bacterial; (4)

dilution of the water by unusually heavy rains; (5) an issue of gas, volcanic or natural; (6) earthquakes or seaquakes." [24]

Then, one by one, he knocked down each. The Everglades had no dead fish. There was a very low concentration of *Peridinium* which he noted, in a prescient memo, as having green color while the large area covered was visible as red, this as yet had not been noted, by any of the fishermen he had talked with. This knocked his original theory for a loop. He then dismissed disease and parasites as a cause due to the periodicity of blooms, arguing that the presence of such vectors would be more prolonged. Dilution was given practically no consideration, because it was an annually recurring event.

When he came to the subject of volcanic gas and seismic activity, he warmed to the topic: "The irregular periodicity, the marine aspect, the area covered, and particularly the limitation to the region concerned all suggest a geological explanation, whether the issue of a gas or the occurrence of an earthquake ...." [25] He continued to embrace the idea that emissions like carbon monoxide (CO), hydrochloric acid (HCI) or ammonium chloride (NH_4CI) could become water soluble, but finally abandoned that line of reasoning. He based this upon an assurance from the U. S. Geological Survey that the west coast of Florida was volcanically inactive, and that he could gather no evidence of the presence of those chemical substances in the water column.

Taylor rather abruptly dismissed the idea of concussive shock as the cause of the fish kill for obvious reasons: lengthy duration of the bloom, southward movement of the biomass and his observation of fish dying while in the live wells of boats. But then his friend, Woodworth, gave some parts of Taylor's analysis new life. He suggested that "unobserved shocks of low intensity could explain the mortality; that occluded gases from the decay from sedimentary organic matter are released by a disturbance to the sediment, under which circumstances the occluded gases would rise into the water, dissolve, and interfere with the life processes of fishes."[26]

Taylor jumped on this idea, setting up a hypothetical scenario based upon Woodworth's suggestions. Water coming down the Caloosahatchee could have been loaded with organic matter given Florida's subtropical climate. As it reached the higher Gulf salinity levels, charged with lime, it would gradually fall to the bottom of the shallow continental shelf and decay anaerobically into methane (CH_4), carbon monoxide (CO), and hydrogen sulfide (H_2S). Over the years, the sediment would gradually build up, until a small seismic shock, undetectable by Woodworth's mechanical devices, would break loose the crust and release occluded gases into the water column. Being organic, he argued they would be water soluble and possess qualities toxic to sea life unaccustomed to those chemicals.

While he came to no definite conclusion, Taylor's work was pioneering. He was a careful and thorough scientist and many of his ideas would be incorporated into later investigations of the red tide and blue-green algae outbreaks of the latter 20th and early 21st centuries. For instance, a bacterium discussed later would show up in vast quantities in releases from Lake Okeechobee, but back in Taylor's time in south Florida, agricultural operations south of Lake Okeechobee responsible for dumping excessive nitrogen and phosphate were decades in the future.

Significance of early reports

The vast number of fish killed, in the 1916 outbreak, was a reminder of that earlier time, when the Gulf of Mexico was an aquatic cornucopia, with virtually unspoiled and abundant aquatic life. Thus, the potential for devastation was that much greater.

The 1916 bloom occurred during the fall. It moved slowly south from Boca Grande to Cape Romano. It existed in both the nearshore and offshore environment. The idea that organic matter would cause toxicity in dinoflagellates and bacteria, and ultimately affect human health, was spot on. Careful autopsies of fish could provide base line data for future scientists and all these factors would become increasingly important as scientists sought to understand the "suffocating gas" in the fall of 1916.

What Taylor's report did not do—somewhat surprising given that he was working for the Commerce Department—was to recommend steps to curb or reduce future outbreaks. But his charge was limited to investigation of the phenomenon, not to venture into palliatives and solutions. Reflecting back on Ernest Ingersoll's report, it can be argued that because the causes of fish die-off were still uncertain, solutions were beyond the reach of the current science.

Reports of fish kills and the scientific analysis that followed the 1916 outbreak were sparse and responsive only to small and localized events. There was little time and effort spent beyond the attempt to describe the visible characteristic of the outbreaks. But based upon the work of Ingersoll and Taylor, science had been introduced into the equation and would become increasingly important as outbreaks grew both temporally and spatially.

The coast of southwest Florida then enjoyed three decades of relative calm, in terms of red tide outbreaks—through the Depression and two world wars—but in 1945-1946, another massive fish-kill hit the state, and this time government authorities awakened to the need for good applied science leading agencies to finally seek possible solutions to a four hundred year-old problem.

CHAPTER 3

Scrambling For Answers

◆———·◆◆··——◆

In the three decades from 1917-1946, with relatively few red tide events, south Florida enjoyed a boom in population. The Sunshine State, boasting mosquito control, air conditioning, low taxes, and a comfortable, active lifestyle, began to attract retirees as full-time residents. Tampa grew from 50,000 in 1915 to 207,000 in 1945; St. Petersburg from 12,000 to 75,000. In 1916, Fort Myers, when Henry Ford purchased his home, "the Mangoes," next door to Thomas Edison's house and laboratory, the population was 3,000; it grew to 12,000 thirty years later.

However, these statistics fail to recognize that additional development took place outside the cities where census data at that time was sometimes unreliable. With a long embrace of individual property rights and privacy, many Floridians saw no reason to be included in early census counts, so the data collected was sometimes woefully inadequate.

Red tide returns

Beginning in 1945, after thirty years of relative normalcy, a series of red tide outbreaks began again along the southwest coast of Florida. The first, in November 1945, was reported by commercial fishermen, local residents and public officials. There were no trained scientists on the scene until January 1946, so early descriptions of the devastation on aquatic life should be taken with a grain of salt.

The bloom began about fourteen miles offshore at Naples, and spread quickly north into Charlotte Harbor, as far as Boca Pass. One report had dead fish scattered all over Fort Myers' beaches at 100 pounds per beachfront foot of sand—an incredible sight. The tidal shore was littered with dead turtles, horseshoe crabs and multiple species of fish from catfish to redfish to snook, indicating that the toxin was throughout the water column and not just at the surface. At its peak, the bloom had a footprint reaching out as far as five to eight miles off Captiva Island on the north, down to Cape Romano below Marco Island to the south.

Concerned by local reports, a science team arrived in late January headed by the eminent G. Walton Smith. British by birth, his academic background was in biology, and the early focus of his work in the Bahamas. In 1940, he joined the faculty at the University of Miami, establishing the International Oceanographic Foundation and a laboratory which would later become the Rosenstiel School of Marine Sciences at the University of Miami. There, his name would adorn the school's main research vessel.

Smith took water samples for laboratory analysis and recorded detailed observations. The samples, however, were not collected until February when the affected area had partly returned to normal, with the northwest winds of winter cold fronts.

The die off from the first bloom devastated benthic invertebrates like shrimp, blue crabs, fiddler crabs and oysters. One report, in March 1946, had eighty per cent of the *Ostrea virginica* oysters growing around the pilings dying quickly. "Clean inner surfaces of their shells, free from any fouling organisms, indicated that death had occurred only recently."[27] There were random reports of fish kills at Key West and Marathon, but no confirmed evidence that the massive red tide made its way through Florida Bay into the Keys.

The second kill began in June 1947. Heavy rainfall for five days, in the middle of the month, produced coastal flooding and excessively heavy runoff from the Caloosahatchee, Myakka and Peace Rivers. However, the water in Charlotte Harbor and the Gulf was not discolored, leading scientists to believe that mortality was due only to the influx of fresh water, with a resulting decrease in salinity, and not to red tide. It also raises the question of septic tanks leaking, because as the water table rose, due to heavy rains, groundwater levels would be pushed upward and the sewage would run into the rivers, near much of the early, residential development. Nearly all the dead fish were thread herring, a species that reproduces and schools in shallow coastal waters. It is possible that they were caught up suddenly by freshwater inundation but were not able to quickly escape. Another likely possibility was that while visually undetected because of high dilution with the heavy rains, there may have been phytoplankton washing into the estuaries, with high levels of toxicity, and the herring, by eating them, would die quickly. Later, confirmed research would show that as cyanobacteria cells from fresh water sources encountered high salinity levels, the external protective armor would deteriorate, leaking deadly toxins into the immediate surrounding environment.

By July 1947, red tide returned with a vengeance. One of the scientists, Paul Galtsoff, described the scene:

" . . . it was learned that the red water first appeared in the waters off Venice and areas to the south about July 6. That colored water first appeared in streaks about 3 to 6 feet wide and one hundred yards long from just off the beaches to 10 miles offshore. It rapidly spread and in about one week was continuous from the beach out to approximately 15 miles offshore. On July 21 observations were made by airplane. Red tide was found from a point halfway up Longboat Key south to Captiva Island. Several runs were made offshore and the infected water at points extended 15 to 20 miles off the beaches. [28]

By the end of the month, the bloom reached the entrance to Tampa Bay, and was moving north, but once it reached Tarpon Springs it stopped, sitting ten to fifteen miles off the shore.

Paul Galtsoff, a collaborator with Walton Smith, had a fascinating life story. Born in Moscow, in 1887, trained as a zoologist, he fled the Bolshevik Revolution in Russia, in 1921, to work for the U. S. Bureau of Fisheries. Two years later, he joined Woods Hole Laboratory, spending much of his time doing field research. He took a doctorate at Columbia University and spent his career studying the effects of various toxins on oysters, including a trip to the Bikini Atoll, in 1946, for testing the after-effects of the atomic bomb.

In his report on the Florida outbreak, he estimated that millions of fish had been killed in three die offs. He reported that "... after several days of winds from off the land, a mass of dead fish was located approximately ten miles offshore from Venice. These fish were packed tightly together in a band 100 to 200 feet wide and extended for miles."[29] Because of the overall number of dead fish, Galtsoff and his team gave up even attempting to estimate the mortality of each species.

However, they did analyze, in great detail, the various plankton found in the water, in an attempt to characterize red tide at the microscopic level. The two most prevalent plankton in the first bloom, not surprisingly, were *Gymnodinium brevis (G. brevis)* and *Trichodesmium*—the former giving a reddish-yellow color to the water and the latter a blue-green tinge, from pigments in the organisms. In the third bloom, *G. brevis* showed up in concentrations of from thirteen million to fifty-six million parts per liter—a remarkable act of reproduction when compared to the starting point at background levels of about one thousand per liter.

The 1945-1947 bloom marked the first time scientists made a concerted attempt to collect samples and do field analysis of the microscopic cells underlying the bloom. This was remarkable because, at the time, the U. S. Fish and Wildlife Service (USFWS) folded into the Department of the Interior, in 1940, had no funds and no personnel to assign to the project. But local congressmen and Florida Governor Caldwell were fervently pleading for federal assistance, as the fishing industry, one of the important economic drivers in Florida's economy, was being financially devastated. With the outcry building, the USFWS was somehow able, with Congressional help, to find funds to recruit and finance some academic assistance to do field studies of the outbreak.

The fact that so much was done in the field pointed to another problem: there was no way to take samples of tainted water into the laboratory, because the microorganisms quickly perished. Laboratory work would be essential to understanding the initiation, growth and termination phases of bloom development. Cultures could be manipulated chemically without damage to the larger ecosystem in which they existed. Field experiments, conducted with the single-minded intention of eradicating microorganisms had a bad history, but would continue, until laboratory cultures of the hundreds of bacteria and algae identified as possible culprits could be reliably grown and reproduced, in a lab beaker or Petri dish.

The Lewisite Scare

Despite impediments at the time, much of the science done on the 1945-1947 outbreak was sound and helpful, but funds cobbled together by the Congress and the USFWS were insufficient to cover much more than little publicized descriptive studies, plus word was getting around that the outbreak was caused by a secret government project. Since anecdotal information passed along rarely retains its original message, the rumor began that the red tide was a direct result of the Department of Defense having dumped mustard gas off the coast of Florida. (The rumor had some factual basis in that the government had dumped some leaking cans off the coast of Mobile, Alabama).

Lewisite was one of two gases developed during World War I, by Lee Lewis. Working in a laboratory at Catholic University in Washington, on arsenic-related chemicals, he came across a student's dissertation describing a combination of arsenic chloride ($AsCl_3$) with dry acetylene (C_2H_2) and aluminum chloride ($AlCl_3$). The toxicity of the products stopped the student from continuing, but Lewis went on to develop large-scale production. The first shipment, from a plant in Willoughby, Ohio, was headed to

Europe in 1918 when the transport carrying it was sunk in the Atlantic Ocean.

Lewisite was regarded as more potent than mustard gas which produced both respiratory and dermatoid stress. It had little odor while mustard gas has a distinct odor, but the two were easily confused by the public, particularly when widespread coughing and nasal and lung irritation were so widespread, especially when walking on or near the beach.

In reality, the only record of dumping mustard gas in the Gulf was the Mobile event in 1947, nearly a year after the 1945-1947 bloom began, but the native suspicion of government secrecy spread through south Florida and the idea that mustard gas was to blame took off like wildfire. This was fueled further by news carried extensively in the local papers of the Nuremberg Code of 1947 describing medical research practices during wartime, bringing further attention to the issue of chemical weapons. The rumor eventually died but this was a reflection of Floridians general distrust of government at almost all levels.

Post-war growth

After World War II, things were changing, some for the better and some for the worse. First, in 1947, the U. S. Army Corps of Engineers (USACE) began the Central and Southern Project for Florida Flood Control and Other Purposes (C&SF)—an ambitious program designed to develop a series of canals, levees, pump stations and retention areas to control the flow of water throughout south Florida. At buildout, there were 720 miles of levees and nearly 1,000 miles of canals, and more than 200 water control structures like pumping stations. One part of the C&SF project included water retention areas and the creation of the Everglades Agricultural Area (EAA), south of Lake Okeechobee, originally designed for 420,000 acres but later expanded to 700,000 acres, to satisfy the state's craving for use of drained land. The southern part of the project was designed to fully hydrate Everglades National Park. Once completed, the federal flood control district was replaced by the South Florida Water Management District.

The second thing that was happening, and the main impetus for the C&SF, was population growth. Between 1940 and 1965, over six million people moved to southern Florida. Miami was growing at the rate of 1,000 people per day, both snowbirds and residents of South American countries, notably Cuba in the late 1950s and early 1960s, seeking to escape despotic political regimes.

And the exurban system of choice for waste disposal was the septic tank. Septic tanks, when installed during the early years, required only that the bottom of the draining area, the drain field, be six inches above the level of the high-water table. In a study of Charlotte County septic tanks, Brain LaPointe of Florida Atlantic University found that over 75% of the older, septic tanks could not meet the new criteria: two feet above the bottom of the drain field.[30] Florida has nearly three million septic tanks; Lee County has over 133,000 ranking second only to Miami-Dade, with over

217,000. And many are old and failing, having been used well past their expected lifetime.

The older tanks are also flirting with the effects of sea level rise. As the water table is pushed upwards, the six-inch gap is being filled with water. Once breached, the human waste, chemicals, pharmaceuticals and bacteria make their way into the groundwater system, eventually flowing downhill into the coastal estuaries, through the porous, limestone substrate that underlies most of coastal Florida.

Much of the problem could be addressed by mandating periodic inspections and pump-outs. A bill passed, in 2010, required regular inspections, but was repealed in 2012, during the anti-regulatory frenzy of Governor Rick Scott, as complaints poured in about the cost of pumping out tanks on a regular basis. Similar bills introduced in the state legislature since then have never made it out of committee to the floor of either the House or the Senate for a vote of the entire legislature . . .

The third change, although hardly noticed, was the permanent location of a scientific research laboratory by the USFWS, in Sarasota, in 1948, as a base for biologists to gather samples and study the periodically blooming waters of the coast of southwest Florida. The lab's work was transferred to Galveston, Texas, in 1952, but the next year a second research station was established in Fort Myers, funded mainly by USFWS and the Florida State Board of Conservation, both alarmed by economic devastation of Florida's commercial fishing industry. Under the supervision of the Galveston laboratory, the Florida station began collecting base line data, on weather, tides and samples of water quality. It moved briefly to Naples, in 1957, and then to St. Petersburg Beach, as the northern boundary of most fish kills to date.[31] Proximity of full laboratory facilities was an important development. Samples taken from coastal areas had a short life, and field analysis was difficult. In addition, labs could experiment on a variety of protocols for control of microalgae without affecting the larger ecosystem.

The important point underlying this was that federal and state governments were finally willing to spend money to assess, and try to prevent, the damage being done to south Florida's commercial fishing economy by red tide outbreaks, and they knew that until good science came into the picture, little would be accomplished. The station conducted aerial surveillance of the most likely red tide bloom areas, from 1949 to the fall of 1952, but could find no outbreaks. As with many government-funded scientific programs, the money flowed toward the most pressing problems (with notable exceptions like the American space program) and began looking toward outcomes that had tangible, measurable economic results—the difference between pure research and applied science—so when phytoplankton outbreaks disappeared the money began to dry up and funds were redirected to other pressing problems.

The 1950s outbreak and a new culprit

After five years of quiescence, blooms came back with a bang. Beginning in November 1952, red tide appeared in a thirty-mile strip—kept some miles off Fort Myers and its beaches by a strong, prevailing northeast wind. The bloom was not consistent in levels of concentration, however, which gave scientists a chance to study various water quality characteristics associated with different levels of bloom intensity. The bloom lasted for only three months and quickly dissipated, as strong cold fronts swept the area in January and February.

But in September, the bloom returned to begin the longest continuous outbreak in south Florida's history. The spatial extent was vast, ranging from St. Petersburg down to Marco Island. By December, the smell was driving people off the beach at Sarasota. One fishing captain reported that he encountered a "yellow mist" rising from the surface causing respiratory distress and nausea to the point where he felt he might pass out. [32]

At Little Marco Pass in April 1954, baby tarpon were seen floating down the Caloosahatchee River, belly up. The tarpon was one of the high-level predators and the last to feel the effect of toxic algae, indicating the extent and severity, of the 1952-1955 bloom.

A careful study of the event, by the University of Miami, points out the state of scientific research at the time. Using a massive number of anecdotal observations from fishing captains to citizens, as well as periodic transects with research vessels, the scientific team separated the outbreak into seven defined geographic zones. These were from the north of St. Petersburg to south of Sanibel Island, to determine the duration and possible surface movement, of high-level concentrations, of the blooms. They hypothesized that the numerous smaller outbreaks, or streaks, were part of a larger underlying phenomenon and that movement was generally from south to north, with a Loop Current eddy as the primary influence. They also thought some of the blooms may have originated inside the coastal passes and were pushed out later into the Gulf by currents. Finally, they sought to correlate outbreaks with lunar cycles, measured against the new moon, noting that the initiation of outbreaks, three days either side of the new moon, never occurred during the study period. [33]

The 1952-1955 outbreak was extensive and deadly. It brought about pressure to find ways to control or eradicate future blooms and two years later, a large-scale experiment was teed up, but only after more study and analysis. The University of Miami study was admirable in detail but misguided as to conclusions. It was one of the best attempts to date to assemble reliable data but fell short. That would have to wait for another forty years.

Herding cats

In an aside to the main bloom, Robert Hutton, a member of the study team and a Department of Conservation scientist at the St. Petersburg lab, received a report, in 1955, of a "minor" outbreak of red tide at Ballast Point in Hillsborough Bay, just south of Tampa. But when investigated, the culprit turned out to be another dinoflagellate, *Ceratium furca*, thriving at 17,600,000 cells per liter. *C. furca* had been found around the world but showed up, for the first time in southwest Florida. Similar to *G. brevis*, it was an armored eukaryotic mixotroph capable of existing and reproducing, both asexually and sexually, in a broad range of salinity and temperature. Blooms were red brown in color and spread in areas suffering from eutrophication and further deplete levels of dissolved oxygen. Fish kills occurred by damage to the gills, but observers noted that mullet and minnows could swim through the streaks of toxic water undamaged.

At the time, eutrophication of Florida's inland lakes was not a widespread problem, but would become so in the future, so the Ballast Point outbreak was most likely an isolated incident. However, it did show that yet another phytoplankton existed, in the Gulf, ready to expand under the right combination of conditions off the coast of rapidly growing southwest Florida.

In another case study done at the same time, a team headed by Howard Odum, for whom the Florida Springs Institute is named, used samples collected over a two-year period to study the effects of the nitrogen to phosphorous ratio on cell growth and bloom intensity.

Odum's team found that to kill fish quickly, *G. brevis* cells had to exist at a level of 450,000 per liter, while citing other studies that fish could be killed more gradually at levels as low as 80,000 cells per liter while some smaller species had survived at concentrations of 800,000 cells per liter.

"It seemed clear to the scientists that although occasional bloom patches had extreme concentrations of nutrients (Ketchum and Keen 1948) the usual blooms capable of killing fish are of lesser magnitude and are accompanied by only a slight increase in nitrogen and phosphorous. Suppose that water with 1000 cells/cc *G. brevis* is toxic to fish . . . it is the intense toxicity of the red water that makes the otherwise ordinary growths of importance. The highest cell concentrations reported in extreme blooms (Davis 1948) are about 15 times this figure. The usual bloom of lesser intensity may require only small injections of nutrients to achieve toxic surges in impoverished inter-bloom water already containing sparse populations of *G. brevis*." [34]

A second part of Odum's report included careful measurements of the levels of estuarine nutrients and their sources, the flushing action of tide and current eddies. The main emphasis was on phosphorous—partly because nitrogen levels were low during the bloom periods and partly because the team was testing the hypothesis that phosphorus was the limiting nutrient to the inception, growth and maintenance of red tide. The report then concluded by touching on one of the causes:

"There is a possibility that the increasing multiple pollution of the shallow coastal estuaries and land drainage cited above may be producing a higher incidence of the red tide phenomenon that might otherwise occur. Authorities responsible for control of this pollution should be made aware of this possibility. In addition to other's incentives, pollution control programs might be recommended as an experiment to check the red tide with the realization that a several year lag is to be expected in the effect of this action on the nutrient levels in the polluted bays." [35]

What is interesting here is the use of the word "pollution." While phosphate in its natural state had existed for centuries in the Peace River watershed, it was clear that Odum's team regarded the situation as going well beyond normal evolution. But Odum's work would not end there. It would expand into another phase: spraying copper sulfate to kill algal blooms.

Copper sulfate

In his earlier report, Paul Galtsoff suggested that copper sulfate ($CuSO_4 5H_2O$) might work as a control on red tide. The Bureau of Fisheries lab, in Galveston, decided to try it out, under controlled circumstances, and found it devastated phytoplankton cells, within a short period of time. Emboldened by test results, the Bureau of Fisheries decided to try it out in nature—in 1957, on a thirty-two-mile long bloom off St. Petersburg Beach, near where the research station was located.

The 1957 event had been studied carefully for movement and nutrient loads. It appeared off Tampa Bay in September. It was sighted off Naples, in October, out of the area by November and returned, driven by southeastward winds in late December but the early stage of the bloom off Tampa offered a perfect opportunity for field experimentation, with copper sulfate as the chemical of choice.

The trial had three criteria: cost of spraying, duration of relief from red tide, and mortality of aquatic species. The third was quickly abandoned because of the difficulty of getting good base line data and then carefully gathering post-application samples for comparative purposes. But the first two went active.

The aircraft of choice were crop dusters. Their pilots were accustomed to flying in straight lines, across carefully delineated fields, to place their loads of pesticides and insecticides within the limits of the farm fields, but the Gulf of Mexico was different. The red tide bloom was irregularly shaped, weaving close to the beaches and then moving away, so the Bureau decided to place a large, orange marker on the beach and moor a research vessel out in the Gulf as the demarcation for the duster pilots. Once the load of copper sulfate was exhausted, the marker and vessel would move up to the next segment. The system proved unworkable, because, at times, the bloom was out of sight of the beach and the research craft was needed to sample the results of the spraying. The problem was solved by having a research scientist fly ahead of the duster and drop a single smoke bomb in the middle of the area to be sprayed, allowing the pilot discretion to fly an optimal coverage pattern.

The result was startling. Offshore from the Blind Pass, the concentration of *G. brevis* was 16,550,000 per liter on the surface and 3,880,000 on the bottom. Sprayed on September 29, the count fell to zero in twenty-four hours, after dusting was finished on the 30th. Ten days later it was back at 380,000 cells per liter on the surface and 363,000 on the bottom and was once again lethal to fish. [36] Looking at the data, Howard Odum's finding of concentration levels in constant flux seems correct, because daily totals of samples show wide variability over the two-week period following spraying. But the important conclusion was that while copper sulfate might offer temporary relief to residents and beachgoers from aerosolized brevetoxin, it was not a viable long-term solution and was replete with possible unintended consequences.

Other than a disastrous experiment, the 1957 outbreak served another useful purpose. An abundance of scientists and field equipment, like research vessels, were in south Florida ready to collect base line data on nutrient content stretching over nearly 200 miles of shoreline. Lake Okeechobee had not undergone eutrophication by 1957, and the sample data collected would later prove invaluable as lake releases began to clog the Caloosahatchee River with toxic algae.

Recognition of a long-term problem

What happened between the 1945-1947 bloom and one decade later was a glimmer of recognition of three long-term problems: damage to Florida's commercial fishing industry, the possibility that human health could be affected and ecological devastation of Florida's estuaries. Of the three, the fishing industry was most directly impacted. The State of Florida initially responded by pleading with the federal government for help, but later became directly involved through the Department of Conservation which had contributed $50, 000 to the copper sulfate trial. The federal government was more responsive, and jumped in sooner, partly because of the exposure to red tide and its multiple cousins scattered along the Gulf Coast from Florida to the Mexican border.

Despite the magnitude and extent of *G. brevis* outbreaks at the time, government funding was never reliable. Independent research continued and private grants to scientists were the main means of financial support. Despite the lack of sustained financing, scientists progressed from describing the problem to proposing solutions.

While the science, during the 1950s, was solid, performed by teams of experts and academicians, with Woods Hole Laboratory and the School of Marine Science at the University of Miami, taking a large role in the early studies, it was also done piecemeal. Taking the different parts as whole, progress was made in understanding the red tide bloom phenomenon once it was underway, but the initiation phase remained largely unstudied.

Part of the problem was that the science teams were ephemeral. Members were not permanently engaged in the study of G. *brevis* blooms because they had other areas of interest, and precious little grant money, save that begged from the government and private foundations, was available for research on red tide.

A major impediment to sustained and continuous funding was the fact that outbreaks were sporadic, so assigning personnel and equipment on a standby basis would be a waste of government funds. The move of the laboratory from Fort Myers to Galveston, in 1952, was done for economic reasons which, while sensible from the government's perspective, made a statement about the long-term commitment to what was now clearly a growing long-term problem. Other than coughing and nasal irritation, human health seemed to be little affected, and the tourist economy was just in its nascent stages. If anything was driving interest, it was the commercial fishing industry of south Florida. The blooms spreading out on the Florida Shelf and down into Florida Bay was putting the shrimpers, crabbers and fin fishermen at economic peril.

With economic damage increasing, and the fishing industry pleading for help, the State of Florida's Department of Conservation (a named to be changed five times in the future) took over the U. S. Maritime Service's training station, at Baysboro Harbor in St. Petersburg, in 1955, making it into a small research lab to study Florida's red tide. It started with a staff of two and an annual budget of a little more than $15,000. Two years later, the staff had grown to ten, and it had expanded its work into studying the effects of the dredge and fill of estuaries. This led to the Bulkhead Act of 1957 that allowed local permits, only after each county had established a line delineating the outer physical limit of permissible coastal development.

And with good reason. The tidal fringe, where fresh water meets salt, heavily populated by the safe harbor of red mangrove roots, was the nursery for most species of commercial fish during the early months of their lives. Safe from most predators, nearly 80% of the state's commercially valuable species, including sport fish like snook and redfish, spent their early lives in the mangrove forests of Florida's coasts. The lab also began to study reproduction, growth and diseases of commercially important species like oysters, setting the stage for better management of natural resources and the ecosystem in which they thrived. But the focus on clams and oysters had an underlying purpose: the vast majority of funding for the lab and staff was coming from dredged oyster shell royalties.

The royalty program had been in place since 1923. Dredgers given the license to harvest from approved state waters were required to pay thirty-two cents per ton into both the state's general fund and the Oyster Conservation Fund run by independent trustees who allocated the money into research, and later marketing, of the bivalve. From 1931 to 1974, dredging companies paid over $5 million into the fund. Shell dredging went through a dizzying set of regulatory changes during this period, but the money continued to flow in and supported the work of the marine labs.

Putting the pieces together

In 1964, concerned about the proliferation of unrelated studies from both academia and government laboratories, George Rounsefell (who had been involved in the copper sulfate spraying experiment) and Walter Nelson, in collaboration with the St. Petersburg field station and Galveston laboratory, issued a monograph combining all the reliable data from 292 published and unpublished manuscripts and papers on red tide related to outbreaks along the Florida coast.[37] Those containing quantitative results were coded and processed—punch cards in those days—to provide a manipulatable data base.

Upon reviewing the data, the authors concluded that *G. brevis* could thrive in a wide variety of environmental conditions related to temperature, salinity, rainfall, wind, upwelling levels from the benthic strata of the Florida shelf, irradiance, and nutrient levels. They also picked up on the fact that of the twenty outbreaks covered in their data base, all commenced between August and November, after the rainy season and after the spring blooming of diatoms as a food source. Three of the outbreaks survived through the winter and spring at lower levels of concentration, reaching full florescence as summer conditions prevailed.

The accumulated reports also showed that much of the early anecdotal evidence about blooms covering massive unbroken areas of the Gulf was wrong. Every scientific observer discussed streaks and threads of the blooms, an important point when considering that the biomass of red tide blooms could be separated while thriving, converging at passes between outer islands and pushed out in streaks by currents, wind and tide. Blanket coverage was simply not the case.

Much of the Rounsefell and Nelson report centered on ways to control the growth and spread of red tide, but the weakness of each of these approaches was similar because not enough was known about the initiation phase, in the natural environment.

Interestingly, the report tended to dismiss anthropogenic causes, i.e. sewage and fertilizers, based on the observation that *G. brevis* could survive and thrive in low-nutrient situations.

On prevention of outbreaks, ideas ranged from chemical—raising to a high level inhibitory heavy metals such as copper, to competition—finding other marine organisms that could compete for prey in the food chain, as well as using water quantity and volume control to make dramatic changes in salinity below *G. brevis* tolerable levels. The last idea cited the Caloosahatchee as an ideal candidate for experimentation. But it would, of course, alter the entire ecosystem of an estuary like Charlotte Harbor, for every living aquatic creature. On control of outbreaks once they occurred, the ideas all involved technology from the use of high frequency radio waves to construction of physical barriers to dramatically separate and change the mixing of bay and Gulf waters. This last idea had great appeal to the authors.

This great procession of ideas, including the use of chemical compounds, from changing the pH of the water using calcium oxide (CaO), more commonly known as quicklime, to spreading charcoal dust to inhibit absorption of nutrients by *G. brevis* cells; the introduction of natural microorganisms to attack the red tide and finally, resorting to a laundry list of chemicals, reflecting the advanced optimism, of the age in chemistry, as the solution for nearly all problems.

Looking through the list, it's hard to believe that the fragile, Florida, coastal ecosystem could stand the shock. For example, the authors cited widespread aerial spraying of larvicide—at that time Malathion and later Baytex—on coastal fringe areas to kill mosquito larvae, as use of a chemical with specific targeted effect and no unintended consequences. This method was popular in southwest Florida, until 1987 when the FFWC concluded that the oil from spray was killing snook larvae, in the mangrove forests of the coast. The science had only begun laboratory work in the mid-1950s, when, for the first time, they were able to create cultures of *G. brevis* and other microorganisms for study and experiment. While field work had been ongoing and somewhat productive, experiments in the lab could be done, with no risk to the environment.

Despite whacky ideas, many of which were mentioned but given short shrift by the authors, the Rounsefell and Nelson report was the first attempt to pull together all pieces of disparate and sometimes unrelated research into a coherent whole. Their recommendations were designed to stimulate further discussion. What was lacking, and would not show up for decades, was sufficient funding to study the problem on a coordinated and ongoing basis. The authors expressed it this way, "Above all, a steady level of funding is required. One cannot do excellent basic research if he is required to fire investigators periodically and then hire whatever personnel are unemployed when funds become available." [38]

This would seemingly improve, as the research lab run by the Department of Conservation was turned into the Marine Research Laboratory (MRL), under the Department of Natural Resources, in 1969. It had opened a field station in the Keys to study the spiny Florida lobster, and grown to forty scientists, a little over dozen support staff, and a donated trawler that allowed systematic mapping of the West Florida Shelf from 1965-1967. Little was known at the time about the shelf apart from anecdotal observation.

But by 1971, the state legislature had decided that funds from oyster dredging should no longer be allocated out by statute to research, the kind produced by the MRL, but should be channeled into the State General Revenue Fund. Some counties managed to keep a part of the fees, but three labs were closed, and personnel reduced. In looking over the history of red tides, activity during the period was non-existent, so once again the state began to lose interest in attempting to study—and eventually solve—the red tide problem. This move reflected both the power of the legislature and the failure of state government to address a growing problem that was affecting one of the era's most important economic engines—the commercial fishing industry. However, the argument lost steam because, during the period 1958-1993, regular blooms occurred but were small and localized. Nothing appeared at the level of the 1953-1955 or 1955-1956 blooms.

Coordination of research begins

Then, in 1993, a massive, red tide event began that would last thirty months and attract the money and attention of federal and state government. It led to the establishment of Ecology and Oceanography of Harmful Algal Blooms (ECOHAB), as a nearly permanent source of federal funding, of a program designed to coordinate research across a broad platform of institutions and topics through the country. The government was concerned that harmful blooms were affecting every coastal state in the country, and the program was set up to better delve into the biological dynamics and effects of the blooms. The result would be a major leap in knowledge about the origins and management of red tide events.

The State of Florida did respond to the 1993 crisis when

Governor Lawton Chiles formed the Governor's Commission for a Sustainable South Florida, in 1994, bringing together disparate groups to deal with Everglades' restoration. That same year the legislature passed the Everglades Forever Act. Saving the Everglades was a popular issue politically, supported by a number of wealthy and powerful people. But neither group was formed with the specific task of trying to better understand the coastal problems plaguing southwest Florida.

The formation of ECOHAB was a watershed moment. Research, until then, was both independently conceived and financed, and was carried out on specific problems identified by the scientists themselves or done at the request of government, in response to civic and community pressures. ECOHAB would bring coordination and oversight into the process and organize research into areas that needed further amplification. And by 1993, enough was known about red tide to formulate a fairly complete picture of the initiation, growth, maintenance and dissipation phases of an outbreak, in order to construct a standard model for red tide also known as the "whirling whips."

CHAPTER 4

Whirling Whips

◆———·◆·◆·◆·———◆

Karenia brevis (K. brevis) known as red tide along Florida's Gulf Coast, is one of the oldest of a large, worldwide family of salt-water phytoplankton that shows up as rust-colored to bright red at high levels of concentration.[39] In scientific terms, it is a photosynthetic, eukaryotic dinoflagellate (being eukaryotic simply means it has a membrane surrounding the nucleus of the cell). In simple terms, like most plants, it performs the admirable function of using sunlight to convert carbon dioxide to food while producing oxygen as a by-product. It is also able to use organic matter as a source for energy, giving it a competitive advantage over other organisms in the water.

Worldwide there are approximately 3,400 to 6,000 different phytoplankton, but less than 2%, or sixty to eighty species are toxic or harmful.[40]

As a member of the diverse dinoflagellate family, *K. brevis* has an oval-shaped single celled body measuring between twenty and fifty microns (millionth of a meter) long and ten to fifteen microns wide.[41] By comparison, a human hair, on average, measures about fifty microns. (The human eye cannot see, unaided, an object below thirty-nine microns).

Coming from a combination of Greek and Latin words—*dinos* meaning "whirling" and *flagellum* meaning "whip."—*K. brevis* resembles a bisected yo-yo with the strings both partially chopped off to allow each cell to propel itself through the water both horizontally and vertically, one twisting the cell while the other moves it through the water . . . at the rate of about one meter per hour.

And while small, a *K. brevis* cell is not simple. Its DNA is approximately thirty times the size of the human genome, making it difficult to study at the level of genomic mapping technology, in the early 1990s. This has been partially overcome in recent years, leading to the discovery of at least ten close cousins of *K. brevis*, with slightly modified genotypes.

Given the complexity of unlocking the genetic code, with the technology available at the time, and in an attempt to better understand a recurrent and potentially dangerous phenomenon, the federal government undertook a massive program, in 1992, to study *K. brevis* and other harmful algae devastating coastal communities.[42] Much of the data presented in this book comes from that program, funded primarily by the National Oceanic and Atmospheric Administration (NOAA) and the Environmental Protection Agency (EPA) "to develop an understanding of the population dynamics and trophic impacts of harmful algal species which can be used as a basis for minimizing their effects on the economy, public health, and marine ecosystems."[43] The effort has produced thousands of pages of sound science from both the field and the laboratory.

Home for K. brevis

The West Florida Shelf (WFS) is a shallow-water, geologic formation comprised of a limestone base that extends nearly 200 kilometers off the coast. Punctuated with sinkholes, it is covered by a thin layer of sediment and silt capable of capturing and holding organic detritus that eventually becomes a food source for K. brevis, which exists rather peacefully at between thirty to one hundred kilometers out in the Gulf—in areas relatively low in nutrients like phosphorous and nitrogen.

In their native environment, where they have lived for hundreds of years, the cells prefer a fairly consistent mix of salinity and temperature, despite the fact that they can exist within a wide range of each. They can adapt at 17.5 psu (practical salinity units measured as 17.5 pounds of salt per 1,000 pounds of sea water) up to 40 psu.

The tolerable range of temperature is as low as 4° C up to about 30° C (86 degrees Fahrenheit), with the optimal level about 25° C or about 76 degrees Fahrenheit. Despite the wide range of tolerance, K. brevis has a measured affinity for temperature and salinity at anywhere between 20° C up to 30° C and salinity of 30 psu to 40 psu. [44]

The fact that *K. brevis* originates and continues to exist, in a low nutrient environment like the WFS has led to significant scientific inquiry. Early theory held that the alga settled in the lower levels on the Gulf—the benthic habitat, until some event such as warming water caused it to release and migrate toward the surface. However, later inquiries showed that *K. brevis* is in nearly constant motion even without the stimulus of external forces. Using its flagella, the little, whip-like projections, each cell's behavior is governed by what is known as a diel cycle,[45] (physiological behavior based upon a twenty-four hour clock ingrained in most forms of life on the planet), moving in a vertical migratory pattern within the water column, highly dependent upon inherent circadian rhythms.

That same movement may also be modulated by external factors, such as sunlight (irradiance), encouraging *K. brevis* to migrate toward the surface to "maximize carbon fixation from photosynthesis" during the day, then settle back toward the bottom to take advantage of dissolved nutrients residing in the silt during darker hours.[46] Scientists have found that *K. brevis* has an "inherent UV resistance and robust photosynthetic capability" that allows it to adjust quickly to changes in varying levels of sunlight.[47] Combined with the mobility to move both vertically and horizontally in the water column, this gives *K. brevis* a competitive advantage over other saltwater algae to consume dissolved nutrients, mainly nitrogen, at night at the benthic level of the West Florida Shelf.

A good understanding of this "grazing" ability is important because something called the Gulf of Mexico Loop Current (LC) and surface winds will eventually move the algae away from its normal domicile of the WFS along and toward coastal communities.

But there have to be stimuli other than just current and wind and background levels of nutrients for *K. brevis* to increase its biomass to new levels, through accelerated reproduction. To understand this, we need to examine the life cycle of a red tide bloom, with its four, distinct stages: initiation, growth, maintenance, and dissipation.

Initiation stage

The main question is: to what extent would an increase in the availability of nutrients cause initiation of the reproductive cycle leading to larger blooms that eventually are driven toward the coast of west Florida?

To answer this, we need to delve into a pile of research to examine four interrelated subjects: the Gulf of Mexico Loop Current and Mississippi River "Dead Zone" off the Louisiana coast; the current meander as related to up-welling and down-welling winds; the cross-shelf barrier; and the presence of Sahara Desert dust on Florida's west coast. All four are important because they contribute, in varying degrees, to the early phases of red tide.

A likely source of nutrients in the silt of WFS is detritus resulting from the decay of organic matter—dead fish and zooplankton waste—sufficient to maintain algal life. One theory is that it could be from nutrient laden sediment transported from the Mississippi River delta, and the so-called "Dead Zone" covering thousands of square miles in the northern Gulf, and driven southeast by the ever-shifting Loop Current. The "Dead Zone" is eutrophic, with less than 2 ppm (parts per million) of dissolved oxygen, which is capable of killing any aquatic life that requires oxygen to survive.

Although red tide has been observed for nearly three hundred years, well before the beginning of agriculture in the northern plains and the location of multiple chemical facilities along the lower Mississippi, it is likely that the LC's transport of Mississippi River sediment has contributed at times to the more recent long-term growth of environmental conditions favorable to the maintenance of red tide offshore on the WFS.

The LC originates in the Gulf of Mexico off the Yucatan peninsula, fed by multiple ocean currents, in and around the Caribbean, and flows clockwise northeast toward the center of the gulf, before turning south and exiting. The northernmost position of the current's loop varies over a six to eighteen-month cycle, creating a bewildering variety of countercurrents or eddies, as it moves north and south. In the northernmost position, the current is up near the Louisiana coast at 29° north latitude. (By comparison, Naples is at 27°.) Although the normal flow is east to west, at times it can entrain "Dead Zone" sediment, by moving water from west to east and south along the Florida coast, before exiting into the Straits of Florida. When in its southernmost position, it barely enters the Gulf and moves quickly through the Straits between Cuba and the Keys to the Atlantic Ocean where is caught up in the Gulf Stream. The position of the LC is a critical factor in the initiation phase of red tide blooms.

Mississippi River Plume Theory

One of the more interesting studies contributing to the standard model for bloom initiation was of Mississippi River outflows for 1979-1982.[48] While the normal flow of the river's outfall is westward, along the Louisiana and Texas coasts, during the April to July period, those four years the fresh water moved eastward, helped by winds and a clockwise eddy current off the northern edge, of the Florida Loop Current.

Using satellite sensors to record and measure the optical properties of colored, dissolved, organic matter and chlorophyll, as it migrated through the Gulf, the data showed there was a significant difference in fluorescence between the high salinity areas and low, such as the mouth of the Manatee, Peace and Caloosahatchee Rivers. Chlorophyll levels in the plume were higher than background levels. (Chlorophyll is a proxy for biomass, so the higher fluorescence the greater the concentration of phytoplankton).

Satellite recording of chlorophyll fluorescence was a relatively new area of science and allowed monitoring of changes to the phytoplankton community. In oversimplified terms, fluorescence is simply a way of measuring light at different wave lengths and researchers acknowledged that there was great variability in the data.

Another study of runoff, in 1993, confirmed the plume theory. While limited, the plume theory does two things: first, it introduces exogenous organic and inorganic matter into the various trophic levels of the WFS ecosystem and second, it supposes, without saying, that the toxic chemicals and excessive nutrients that created the Mississippi River "Dead Zone" off the coast of Louisiana could make their way onto Florida's lower west coast and even down into the Florida Keys. To the first point, since *K. brevis* is a mobile dinoflagellate, capable of moving up and down the water column, it could take advantage of the nutrient mixture, to begin the initiation phase of a bloom cycle.

Another study into the initiation phase, as affected by the LC, was undertaken in 1997, by the redoubtable Karen Steidinger and Patricia Tester, of the NOAA National Marine Fisheries Service. Integrating timely data with other studies, they concluded one critical factor involved was the meander (much like weather fronts) of the LC, during the late summer and early fall, which drove *K. brevis* cells from off shore to near shore where a substantial dose of nutrients and land-based runoff was available to feed the bloom. [49]

This was an important breakthrough in determining how the red tide phenomenon might be predicted, and became the subject of a follow-up study, published in 2015, confirming the original conclusion. [50] Using data from

1954 to 2009, they examined only large blooms, defined as those with a concentration of cells at 100,000 per liter (the threshold number at which red tide becomes visible to the human eye and becomes toxic to animal life and human health) or higher, with regard to other variables, one of which was the importance of wind direction creating up-welling and down-welling outcomes on the WFS.

Up-welling and down-welling winds

For coastal science studying the movement of water, there are two kinds of atmospheric forcing winds: up-welling and down-welling. The former tends to move water toward the coast while pushing nutrients from the lower levels upward toward the surface, while down-welling winds push warmer surface water, with dissolved oxygen, from the coast down to the lower levels of the Gulf. In the area studied, wind direction varies seasonally, and large blooms tended to be related to northerly winter up-welling winds.

If the LC was in the southern position, *K. brevis* cells did not have the potential to bloom, because the LC drove benthic-level nutrients toward the surface, with mixing favoring other fast-growing phytoplankton that could outcompete the "grazing" preference of *K. brevis*. After periods of no blooms, by down-welling winds and after almost twenty years of careful study, researchers have concluded that the LC has to be in the northern position for a bloom to occur but when it is, the upwelling winds form a powerful convector of nutrients.

Cross shelf barrier

Another wind-related factor is the cross shelf barrier, a dynamic zone on the southern end of the WFS. It moves seasonally, blocking the movement of the LC while creating an area of differing salinities and temperatures. The barrier moves toward the coast but is persistent. On the landward side, the water becomes stratified, preventing mixing and favoring the grazing behavior of *K. brevis* in competition with other diatoms in the water column, as nutrients from urban runoff and agriculture cluster at the cross shelf barrier.

Catnip for Karenia

An important piece of the initiation phase puzzle was uncovered by John J. Walsh and Karen Steidinger, after studying the history of Saharan dust, with iron in it, when compared to red tide outbreaks along the southwest Florida coast, over a period of five years. Gathering summer wind and rainfall data from Tampa to Fort Myers, they found that the level of airborne dust particles measured at Miami correlated with rainfall amounts measured at Venice each year from 1992-1996, with massive red tide outbreaks in 1994 and 1995.

The appearance of Saharan dust is dependent upon the strength and timing of the El Niño/Southern Oscillation—an atmospheric phenomenon that allows warmer water to move westward in the Pacific Ocean toward North America pushed by the Equatorial Current. So, under the right conditions, as low-pressure systems move from Africa toward the Florida coast, they contain both dust and moisture. Saharan dust consists in part of diatoms, a single-celled alga, with a silica wall. As it is deposited in the Gulf by heavy rain, it feeds a bacterium called *Trichodesmium*, which in turn uses the iron in the dust to convert or "fix" nitrogen into aquatic consumables, mainly ammonia, for any algae in the neighborhood. And, recalling its mobility and omnivorous "grazing" behavior, it's likely that *K. brevis* would take full advantage leading some scientists to conclude that particulate iron, deposited by heavy rains on the west coast of Florida, accelerated outbreaks as long as it is considered with other factors.[51] The Saharan dust theory is still being studied because initiation is the most difficult phase to hypothecate, in the four life stages of a bloom.

Initiation phase model

In conclusion, the initiation phase can be stimulated by a combination of factors. First, the loop current needs to be in a northern position. Second, winds from the north tend to create nutrient-rich upwelling water along the WFS and coastal areas. Third, with Saharan dust containing iron stimulates, *Trichodesmium* may create an enriched nutrient inventory. Fourth, watershed runoff of agricultural fertilizers and urban runoff mainly from old and failing septic tanks pours down the rivers and empties into coastal estuaries. All four do not necessarily have to be present; at least two or three are sufficient to set the table for a smorgasbord of nutrient-rich water for the omnivorous and opportunistic *K. brevis*.

Growth stage

Once nutrients become available in sufficient quantity, in a water column suitable for the adapted grazing behavior of its cells, *K. brevis* enters its growth stage by rapidly increasing biomass.

For a better understanding of how *K. brevis* can compete with faster growing phytoplankton and diatoms, we also need to understand the reproductive cycle. *K. brevis* reproduces both asexually and sexually. As cells grow from a background concentration of less than 1,000 cells per liter, they double by asexual binary fission cell division increasing geometrically, that is one cells becomes two, two four, four becomes eight . . . *ad infinitum*. The rate of division varies but averages approximately one-third of the cells per day. The increasing level of biomass, depending upon the growth medium and conditions, begins to create depleted oxygen zones in the area of the bloom, affecting other marine species where death and decomposition of marine life near the bloom begins a vicious cycle to further reduce oxygen levels, until the bloom becomes large enough to begin to move toward the coast of Florida.

One question that plagued scientists was: how does a slow reproducing alga compete for food sources against other faster-growing plankton and phytoplankton? In the natural world, competition determines which species survive and which do not. The Darwinian view of biological fitness, or the ability to pass along through the reproductive process those genotypes that best serve the population, is in play even at the microscopic level of diatoms and algae, and are two factors where *K. brevis* excels: the ability to do damage to its competitors and the broad range of nutrients that can be consumed by red tide.

The first factor is allelopathy—the ability to produce and release compounds toxic to competitors. In a study published in 2005, a laboratory experiment exposed induced allopathic compounds at various levels to phytoplankton competitors. Two of the three Gulf of Mexico species exposed had reduced concentrations and slower growth rates (as did *K. brevis* cells to a lesser extent) and one was unaffected.[52] This form of chemical aggression may explain the survival rate of nascent red tide, in the early growth stage of a bloom.

The second is ability to adapt to a wide variety of nutrients . . . In 2014, after considerable research into the subject, Mote Marine published the following list:

Undersea sediments
Decaying fish
Water flowing out of estuaries
Deposits from the atmosphere
Nitrogen from the air "fixed" into a more useable form by
   the naturally occurring bacteria Trichodesmium.

Waste from zooplankton – small aquatic animals visible to the human eye.

The "grazing" of smaller zooplankton dubbed "micro zooplankton" because they can only be seen under a microscope.

Picoplankton – tiny life forms that *K. brevis* consumes

Bacteria transforming nitrogen in the water into more useful forms

Light creating available nutrients from natural, dissolved compounds like tannins in the water

Decay of Trichodesmium blooms

Nitrogen from the air "fixed" by other cyanobacteria that are NOT Trichodesmium. [53,54]

It also helps explain why red tide is able to grow its biomass as it moves from offshore to onshore pushed by wind and currents throughout the water column (mainly on the surface), because clearly red tide is able to extract from, utilize, and consume a broad array of nutrients.

The ability of *K. brevis* to utilize this broad variety of microbes, bacteria, marine invertebrates, fish, plant and animal life makes it a brutal competitor, in the Gulf of Mexico. It is a mixotroph, meaning its cells can use both organic and inorganic sources to sustain life and reproduce. Many other phytoplankton are autotrophs—meaning they can use inorganic sources like photosynthesis—sunlight and carbon dioxide to create sugars and generate energy.

They then become fodder for mixotrophs or heterotrophs—organisms like human beings that depend upon organic matter for sustenance.

Finally, the growth stage, generally defined as moving from 5,000 to 20,000 cells per liter, is fueled primarily by nutrient availability. It also depends upon a proper combination of salinity, temperature and irradiance—all of which determine the extent to which the bloom expands and at what rate. While there is wide tolerance for all factors, preference is for higher salinity in the Gulf of Mexico, but as the blooms move eastward, they are driven into coastal waters with lower salinity and bountiful nutrients, from fresh water runoff of rivers, lakes and anthropogenic waste.

Maintenance phase

As a bloom moves toward the Florida coast, it begins the third stage of life, now depending upon new sources of nutrients, conveniently provided by land-based runoff of agricultural and lawn fertilizers like nitrogen, phosphorous and failing septic tanks.

There are major differences in south Florida's coastal waters as to the amount present of either phosphorous (P) or nitrogen (N). The atomic ratio between the two in the world's oceans is expressed as a ratio of 16:1—that is sixteen-parts N to one-part P. That also happens to be the ratio of phytoplankton, which makes the oceans an ideal environment where there are sufficient nutrients. The most productive areas tend to be along the west coast of continents, as the upwelling west to east winds push nutrient-rich deeper water upward toward the land.

In Florida, the west coast tends to be rich in P. This is due in part to the natural runoff from mining operations along the Peace and Myakka Rivers combined with agricultural runoff. For example, if the N:P ratio of coastal waters is 16:2, then the phytoplankton will absorb, or uptake, at the normal rate of 16:1 leaving no N but one parts of P remaining. This is known as a "nitrogen limited" area.

In addition, during the El Niño summers, phytoplankton increases in the Gulf of Mexico as increased rainfall lead to more runoff from the land. Research indicates that *K. brevis* dominates, at bloom concentrations, the near offshore coastal area from Tampa Bay down to Charlotte Harbor, an area with the lowest organic and inorganic N:P ratio along the west coast. Moving south past Cape Romano and further out in the Gulf, the dominant algae are cyanobacteria, with the N:P ratio gradually changing. Finally, moving down into Florida Bay, the dominant phytoplankton are diatoms—microscopic and ubiquitous, free-floating, unicellular, aquatic algae being blown around by the wind and ocean currents—in a "phosphorous limited" area since much of the land-based runoff heavily nitrogen-loaded comes from the Everglades Agricultural Area down through Everglades National Park and the ratio is more like 32:1.[55]

While either a chronic or an episodic supply of nutrients is required for high biomass, the bloom has the ability to regenerate and recycle nutrients, necessary as the ambient forms are consumed and absorbed into the growing biomass. In addition, during the maintenance phase, similar to the earlier growth initiation stage on the WFS, rapid cell proliferation creates pockets of dissolved oxygen in close proximity to the bloom, leading to death and decomposition of marine life. And not all runoff needs to directly stimulate red tide growth; it can expand to other elements of the food web which ultimately benefits the omnivorous and varied appetite of *K. brevis.*

Another nearshore source, recently discovered, is cyanobacteria discharged from rivers along the west coast of Florida. The Caloosahatchee is a prime example of how the system works. As the polluted water of Lake Okeechobee pours down toward Charlotte Harbor, loaded with blue-green algae, bacteria enters the estuary with its higher salinity and begins to die off, with the residue becoming available to the more salinity tolerant algae sitting off the coast. It is, in fact, the perfect storm, as the fresh water cyanobacteria invades canals and coastal estuaries, while eventually nourishing red tide sitting just off the coast.

Dissipation

Red tide blooms have, since the early 1970s, become more frequent and they stay longer and now are annual events. Maximum levels of cell concentrations have extended their lives over the period of a bloom, while peak levels have remained the same, in the range of 10 million per liter generally expressed as 10^7—a far cry from the background concentrations of 1,000 or 10^3 per liter.

Natural forces that dissipate a red tide bloom are the same ones, by their absence, that initiated and maintained cell growth: wind, tide, rainfall and nutrients. However, these factors taken independently are growing less important as the appearance of blooms has both strengthened and lengthened. Two-thirds of all blooms move onshore between September and November, the beginning of Florida's "dry season" when rainfall becomes scarce to non-existent, reducing lower salinity fresh water along the coast and reducing the need for discharges, from an engorged Lake Okeechobee, with its failing Hoover Dike.

As the wet season ends, afternoon offshore winds, driven by Everglades-originating thunderheads, abate and northwest winds accompanying northern cold fronts begin to prevail. With these fronts come cooler weather and the Gulf temperature drops from the range of 26° C down to around 15° C.

The dissipation phase, driven by natural forces including extreme situations such as hurricanes, is the least well understood part of the *K. brevis* life cycle. Because blooms now last longer in greater concentrations, and because natural factors other than a reduction in nutrients tend to work in favor of red tide near shore blooms, it's possible that the background location and concentration of the dissipated cells remain on the WFS closer to shore, ready to bloom again when conditions are right.

Yes—there are more

K. brevis is not the only saltwater phytoplankton to plague the west coast of Florida. *Trichodesmium*, discussed earlier, is a cyanobacterium that serves as a food source for red tide. Growing on the surface of the Gulf, it congregates in large chunks that look like small wood shavings or foam and "fixes" nitrogen, meaning that it absorbs inorganic nitrogen (N_2) gas from the surface and turns it into organic nitrites (NO_2), nitrates (NO_3) and ammonia (NH_3)—all fertilizers for red tide initiation and growth. This saltwater bacterium is one of the primary causes of red tide blooms supported by the fact that *Trichodesmium* blooms normally occur from May to September, while *K. brevis* blooms generally make an appearance from September through November

Another visible phenomenon is "true" brown tide, known scientifically as *Aureoumbra lagunensis*, found generally in the Caribbean and identified as far north as the Indian River Lagoon, on the east coast of Florida. But now *Cylindrotheca*, a bloom similar in color, and causing multiple aquatic species to die and wash up on southwest Florida beaches, is beginning to appear. A fast-growing diatom, it floats feely with wind and tide and tends to appear near shore, with northwest winds and high tides. While not toxic to human beings, it is deadly on marine life like grass eels, flounder and blue crabs, all of which exist at the lowest levels of the bottom—the benthic habitat—and all of which suffocate due to a lack of dissolved oxygen. Lee County recently experienced another brown-colored bloom caused by a species of the genus *Peridinium*, another motile freshwater dinoflagellate, possibly originating in Lake Okeechobee and floating down the Caloosahatchee River.

While some of the blooms described are visible to the narrow range of the human eye, microscopic examination of the individual cells show a much wider range of color, from burgundy to yellow. The appearance of red tide as "red" is more a result of high biomass and photosynthetic pigments producing an image in the human eye that is not necessarily the actual wavelength of the cells.

There is one more alga—actually a bacterium—that will become the major concern, with human health worldwide. Covered more extensively, in later chapters in this book, it will appear gradually beginning in southwest Florida in the late 1980s. While billions of years old, and foundational to all life on this planet, particularly humans, it has been in Florida in background presence and concentrations since before the land mass separated from Pangea. But, since water control systems were put in place in Lake Okeechobee in the late 1940s, it has grown to massive concentrations, causing economic damage and potential human health problems beyond the more familiar *K. brevis*.

Scientists have concluded that there are twenty-eight different cyanobacteria present in Lake Okeechobee, but the most abundant, and the most dangerous to animals and long-term human health, to which we now turn, is *Mycrosistis aeruginosai*, more popularly known as guacamole sludge.[56]

CHAPTER 5

Holy Guacamole

◆────· · ◆ · ·────◆

On a cool, February morning in 2019, with the wind blowing hard out of the east down the Caloosahatchee River, we are looking for signs of blue-green algae with Captain John Cookman and his wife Kathy.

"I can't believe we're doing this goin' up river," he said "because it's February and I can't remember ever seeing algae this time of year, but it was here yesterday right off the east edge of Franklin Lock and Dam."

"We ought to be going down to the Orange River," says Kathy, "Last week there were at least a hundred manatees down there. Yesterday there were maybe a dozen. They're moving out because the water is so warm that they don't need to sit in the power plant outflow anymore." The Orange River is a discharge canal used by Florida Power and Light, and for years has been the gathering place for the giant sea cows when temperature in the Gulf falls below 68° Fahrenheit.

John Cookman and his wife are salty, genial folk. Steeped

deeply in history and natural science, they run a small company out of Sweetwater Landing, near Fort Myers. Kathy offered a little history. "We came down here and bought this company because I had worked for twelve years in the Columbus Zoo, with the three manatees that lived there, and I developed this passion for the species. So, when we came here, we decided to find a way to educate visitors in the ecology of southwest Florida, and that's what we try to do every day."

But the Caloosahatchee River ecosystem has been brutally battered by pulse releases of toxic water from Lake Okeechobee, as the U. S. Army Corps of Engineers seeks to protect the failing Hebert Hoover Dike, surrounding the lake from breaching.

As we go through the Franklin Lock, John comments, "I can remember back in the '70s when you could see right to the bottom of this river. It was sandy, maybe five or six feet deep. Now, you can hardly see three feet." He lowers a Secchi disc and pulls it up quickly.[57] "So, there you see it—about two feet eight inches."

The lock separates salt from fresh water in the Caloosahatchee. While the turbidity remains the same, plant life is remarkably different. On the up river side of the lock, various aquatic plant like duckweed and pennywort proliferate, fed by phosphorous and nitrogen. On the down river side, the shoreline and oxbows are fringed with mangroves and McMansions.

The wind has dispersed the blue-green algae, so we

go back through the lock and head for the marina. Asked at what temperature things begin to change, both John and Kathy need to think for a moment. "I think the magic number might be 70°, he replied, "but then just to be safe, I'll say 68°. That's the point where the cyanobacteria sink down into the water column and isn't visible from the boat. It's also the point at which manatees decide to move out to the Gulf."

Kathy chimes in. "There are no more seagrasses in the river. You know the manatee has to eat about one-tenth of its body weight each day, so they need to find places where they can satisfy their need to feed. A lot of folks have tried to plant seagrasses in the river, but they never seem to take. It probably has to do with the releases cleansing out the bottom of the river, or it may have to do with the cyanobacteria, but if there are no grasses there are eventually going to be no manatees."

Blue-green algae

Cyanobacteria are one of the oldest forms of life on earth. The evidence is embedded in stromatolites, or mounds and layers of calcareous matter containing bacteria, found from the pre-Cambrian era and through the Cambrian explosion. Marine animals and other life forms used cyanobacteria as an ongoing but depletable source of nutrition. The ubiquitous presence of the bacteria has led some researchers to believe that about 2.4 billion years ago, cyanobacteria may have played a large role in what is known as the Great

Oxygenation event, when atmospheric oxygen rose from 1% to today's level of 21%, allowing it to kill off many of its econiche competitors existing at the time.

Cyanobacteria comes in multiple genetic strains but can be generally characterized as a microscopic unicellular prokaryote. Being a prokaryote, it lacks an external membrane (but has a thick and gelatinous cell wall), with no distinct nucleus or specialized organelles (little specialized structures within the cell), whereas a eukaryotic dinoflagellate like *K. brevis* has both a clearly defined membrane and nucleus. The outer band of mucilage holds the cell together, until it deteriorates and eventually releases the organelles into the water column.

Cyanobacteria has no obvious means of mobility but, has gas vesicles that allow them to adjust buoyancy to ambient irradiance while being able to consume both nitrogen and carbon dioxide, to produce oxygen as a byproduct. Being photosynthetic, they are now considered to be algae.

Some cyanobacteria work together cooperatively. One method used to encourage gathering is the presence of cells known as heterocytes that take inorganic nitrogen from the atmosphere and convert it into more usable forms like ammonia and organic nitrogen, allowing colonies to exist where the supply of nitrogen would normally be insufficient to support a large biomass. This abundance of nutrition attracts other cells and, when of sufficient concentration, becomes the green mats that cover backwater bays and other areas where there is little mixing.

Cyanobacteria, like dinoflagellates, reproduce in a number of ways, the most straightforward being cell division based upon duplicated DNA. They have the ability to double the population every two days, under ideal conditions.

Most of the strains are benign, but some are not. When in high concentration levels, they become toxic to all forms of life, including humans. *Mycrosystis aeruginosa* and *Anabaena circinalis* are the two most prevalent in Lake Okeechobee, with the former being the most prevalent. The toxins come in four categories: neurotoxins, dermatoxins, hepatotoxin and general skin irritation. While existing quietly in healthy cells, once the outer membrane is ruptured or otherwise disturbed, toxins leach out into the aqueous environment and are instantly water soluble. All four have a long half-life and can survive for weeks, sometimes for months. They are fast-acting, and the effects depend entirely upon the level of concentration.

So, how did these truly ancient microorganisms, having have survived early environmental challenge throughout the planet's history, and forming one of the building blocks of life on this planet, become a threat to human health in south Florida? To best understand the origins of the problem, we need to look back to the history of the draining of the Everglades.

History of Lake Okeechobee

As homo sapiens began to spread across south Florida six thousand years ago, those newcomers who did not live on the coast, with abundant fish and oysters, hunted an inland population of large mammals, including saber-toothed tigers and large mastodons as a source of sustenance. They also encountered a slow-moving swamp between the two coasts, over a hundred miles long, running from the Kissimmee Lakes area, down between the Sha-Na-Legee ledge, bordering today's Big Cypress Swamp on the west and the South Atlantic Coastal Strip to the east, with an elevation change of less than twenty feet. It was later dubbed affectionately by Marjorie Stoneman Douglas as "the River of Grass."

Lake Okeechobee had originally been a giant holding pond for the River of Grass, fed by a large swath of land beginning south of the present city of Orlando, where water oozed, at the rate about one-half mile per day, from the Kissimmee Lakes down into Florida Bay.

As the Anglo-Europeans moved in, they regarded the North American continent as an opportunity to create a new Eden—comprised of small farms growing enough food to feed the new nation—the vision of Thomas Jefferson. The Swamp and Overflowed Lands Act was passed by Congress, in 1850, giving states the right to claim any land, in its natural state, unfit for agriculture. Florida, having been granted statehood only five years earlier, took full advantage, claiming twenty million acres of swamp as state lands. Then, in 1855, the state created the Internal Improvement Fund (IIF), overseen by the governor and four members of the cabinet, to decide how to put the land to the best and highest use, a refrain to be repeated through the present day.

The IIF saw the fastest way to develop the state was to bring in railroads, but so much money and effort was being spent on opening the American West that the rail companies had little use for the mosquito-infested and hurricane-prone state, occupying the country's southeastern fringe.

In 1881, a Philadelphia developer, Hamilton Disston, cut a deal for four million acres of swampland, for which he would drain another twelve million acres of state land. If successful, he would acquire one-half of the drained land—which happened to be the River of Grass—an area covered by a rich muck—ideal for farming.

The scheme never worked but was doubled down by Governor Napoleon Bonaparte Broward, who ran on a platform of draining what he called "The Empire of the Everglades." Broward found an engineer from the U. S. Department of Agriculture named James Wright, who planned and began an effort to drain the Everglades in 1908. The project quickly ran out of money and Broward attempted to recover some of the losses by selling 500,000 acres to developers.

Unfortunately, the new owners took to heart the analysis done by Wright, which was fatally flawed. It underestimated the amount of rainfall, during periods of inundation, throughout the summer months and began touting it as an investment opportunity. The price of land was skyrocketing, but reports began to circulate that Wright's figures were wrong leading the market to collapse, followed by a series of lawsuits, indictments and other forms of recrimination.

Despite all the excitement about development, farming had begun to take hold on a workable scale in sections where the drainage could be carried out easily and where water was abundant—around the southern border of Lake Okeechobee—sponsoring a number of small towns like Clewiston, Belle Glade and Moore Haven. The crops included sugar cane, which had been grown south of the lake, since around 1890. Then, in 1926, a hurricane hit south Florida and the dirt levee protecting Moore Haven collapsed, as the result of bad planning and execution, resulting in four hundred drownings. Two years later, the same story repeated itself, as that fall, another storm blasted through the state killing thousands, many of whom lived in the town of Belle Glade and were migrant workers brought in to work the crops being grown in the Everglades.

The devastation brought President Herbert Hoover, an engineer by training, to the scene. Promising it would never happen again, he got Congress to appropriate funds for the U. S. Army Corps of Engineers (USACE) to build an eighty-five-mile dike, along the southern edge of the lake. The original project would later grow into a one hundred forty-three-mile long levee, surrounding much of the lake's perimeter. It expanded gradually, as was the Corps' wont, into a water management and control system for the benefit of agricultural interests.

The nation soon plunged into the Great Depression and

while the urban population throughout the country was marginalized, farming operations south of Lake Okeechobee thrived. South Florida was spared serious hurricane damage, for the next fifteen years, but was plagued by droughts at the end of World War II, until 1947, when Miami recorded over one hundred inches of rainfall, twice the annual average, leading Congress to authorize the Corps to build the Central and South Florida Project for Flood Control and Other Purposes (C&SF). The magic words, for purposes of analyzing the cause of the massive cyanobacteria outbreaks beginning four decades later, were "Other Purposes."

The project took twenty years to complete. It covered 15,000 square miles and eighteen counties in south Florida. Land set aside for agriculture immediately south of the lake, the EAA, now produces row crops and sugar cane. The cane industry, populated by small farmers, in the years after the Hoover Dike was built, consolidated into an industrial agriculture conglomerate known as U. S. Sugar. The company had a checkered history, in the early years, being indicted for peonage (a modified form of slavery), in federal court, but the charges were dismissed on a technical point. By the 1960s, President Reagan placed an embargo on Cuban goods flowing into the U.S. to economically squeeze the Castro regime and Cuban interests. The Fanjul family, having emigrated to the U.S., bought land in the EAA to expand their vast cane sugar operations, from the Caribbean to south Florida, with a company titled Florida Crystals.

In the EAA, both vegetables and sugar require nitrogen

and phosphate. With hundreds of pumps and a large lake nearby, Okeechobee enabled growers to operate year-round, by moving water south in the dry season and serving as a receptacle for back-pumped water, when it was no longer needed for crops. Between 1960 and 1968, acreage used for growing cane sugar quadrupled. Later between 1973 and 1978, the amount of phosphorous runoff generated from both industrial farming operations in the EAA and cattle ranching and dairy cows from the Kissimmee River watershed doubled, with the result that from 1973 to 1983 the amount of nitrogen and phosphorous in Lake Okeechobee also doubled. While some of the nutrient-laden water was sent down the St. Lucie and Caloosahatchee Rivers to the Indian River lagoon and Charlotte Harbor, much of it remained, sinking slowly toward the bottom to create a legacy that would haunt the coastal estuaries, in the years to come.

In addition to an environmental disaster, the State of Florida was about to create a bureaucratic nightmare—joint management of Lake Okeechobee split between the USACE and the South Florida Water Management District (SFWMD).

The district was first created, in 1949, as the Central and South Florida Flood Control District, a way of attempting to coordinate the state's effort with the C&SF project underway. That was followed by creation of five water management districts, in 1972, with passage of the Florida Water Resources Act, a brilliant piece of legislation that created governmental entities based upon watersheds and not the normal geopolitical boundaries. However, there were two flaws: first, members of the governing board would be appointed by the governor, with certain specifications, which always led to "follow the money" to find out who might be appointed; second, it was one of the extremely rare instances where taxing power was granted to a non-elected body.

The joint oversight problem was not apparent from the beginning. The quantity and timing of water releases to control the overall lake level was vested in the Corps, as set forth in the Lake Okeechobee Release Schedule (LORS), subject to periodic review and revision.

Control of agricultural leases, with related issues of water use coming in and out of the lake to farms, and the quality of the water was within the purview of the SFWMD. The District had a multiplicity of other responsibilities such as the issuance of consumptive use permits and approval of development projects, as did the Corps with its required approval of development plans through 404(d) permitting, but the bottom line was that management of water in and out of the lake came down to a split jurisdiction where quantity was controlled by USACE and quality the responsibility of the SFWMD.

Beginning to control agricultural operations

By 1986, the State of Florida issued a set of stringent regulations mandating that waste from dairy farms had to be maintained and processed, within the boundary of the farm. It came at great expense to the farmers, but recycling of waste into fertilizer mitigated the cost somewhat. The program included a buyout of thirty-two of the fifty-one dairy farms at the time. One interesting aspect of the unusually harsh rule was timing, because the first discovery of deadly toxins from Lake Okeechobee occurred in 1987 and again in 1989.[58] In a similar scenario to the earliest discovery of red tide, it was dead cattle near Lake Okeechobee and complaints by residents of skin irritation, after coming in contact with tainted water, that alerted authorities to a potential problem. The problem had existed all over the world, but this was the first manifestation of human health issues, resulting from cyanobacterial contamination in south Florida.

The nutrient load from the EAA and pasture operations in the Kissimmee Lakes area had created a legacy of nitrogen and phosphorous that would never be overcome, eventually feeding the colonies of dinoflagellates migrating from the West Florida shelf, and by poisoning the lake to a level where eutrophication was inevitable. Whether this was done through ignorance of the long-term consequences of watershed management or an insatiable appetite for agricultural land fed by lobbying money, from the sugar industry, with its government subsidies, mattered little, until the Hoover Dike began to fail.

In 2006, Hurricane Katrina slammed into New Orleans devastating the lower 9th ward as dikes and levees collapsed and the Mississippi River Gulf Outlet underperformed, in its role as a diversionary canal. The catastrophe caused the Corps to examine all structures protecting population centers, and when it came to the Hoover Dike, it was declared in "grave and imminent danger" of failing. Originally designed to hold water up to eighteen feet deep, the Corps decided to maintain levels at somewhere between twelve and a half and fifteen and a half feet. This caused a change in the LORS but with little public notice given the emergency situation at the time.

By 2006, the lake had undergone vast changes. The 730 sq. mi. water body had been inundated with nitrogen and phosphorous from the 700,000 acres of farm fields, 65% of it from cane sugar, controlled by two giant industrial agricultural operations: U.S. Sugar and Florida Crystals' and while the dairy farmers north of the lake had been struggling, since 1986, to keep all animal waste within farm boundaries, cattle ranching had few restrictions and their herds were allowed to freely pollute the groundwater system, with the result that the level of existing phosphorous rose from thirty parts per billion (ppb) to one hundred twenty ppb in the 1990s. In addition, there was the hardening of the bottom muck in the lake, a layer estimated to comprise fifty million tons of phosphorous at the benthic level.

Releases by the Corps from the lake, occurred on an irregular, but frequent, basis from 2006 on. The deadly toxins, *Mycrocystis* and *Anabena*, were capable of killing cattle and creating skin irritation on humans, in contact with the polluted water. The World Health Organization had recognized the deadly nature of both strains and set guidelines for consumption, but little was made of it in the State of Florida.

As the problem became more apparent to property owners along the coastal bays and constructed canals, a research project showed that as the cyanobacteria was carried by releases down the Caloosahatchee River, saltwater would erode the gelatinous shell releasing toxins directly into the water. In an article published in 2018, the author asserted that "dilution is the solution" assumed by water management authorities to be a palliative was invalid, because, with large concentrations, the algae had the ability to form massive levels of scum at the surface to choke off non-buoyant algae.[59]

The scum forms into a solid crust which, under the right circumstances, releases the top layer into the air. In another 2018 study performed by Florida Gulf Coast University (FGCU) and funded by NOAA, researchers found that airborne particles of microcystins could travel up to one mile inland, in low concentrations. Researchers are checking for the presence of the aerosolized toxin up to three miles inland, but the particles would likely be at an extremely low level. Arguably, the presence of the toxin so far inland could be at a background level, but the researchers concluded that the particles could possibly travel up to one mile inland.[60]

In summary, the 1947 C&SF project created a drainage

and water management system south of the lake that led to intensified industrial agricultural operations, in which the demand for water, both in and out of the fields on a timely basis, was deemed essential to crop growth and harvest. The inflow of nitrogen and phosphorous from the EAA combined with cattle and dairy operations in the Kissimmee River watershed eventually led to pollution of the lake where conditions were ideal for the growth of large colonies of cyanobacteria.

Cyanobacteria are probably the reason why we, the human species, are here but they need to be treated with caution in today's world, as we have altered forever the balance of nature. And south Florida is an example of how the mismanagement of natural resources has turned one of the building blocks of life into a potential monster. All this would begin to coalesce, as salt-water algae blooms swept in from the West Florida Shelf, to combine with the twenty-eight different species of cyanobacteria being pushed down the Caloosahatchee Rived, by pulses of nutrient laden water. [61] The on again and off again process would become a regular event in 1994 and the State of Florida began to take notice.

CHAPTER 5

Coming to Grips

◆——— · ● ◆ ● · ——— ◆

Records of red tide outbreaks have been kept, at various degrees of detail, since 1878. The most complete is compiled by the Florida Fish and Wildlife Research Institute (FWRI), in St. Petersburg. With over 600 employees, it is funded by user fees, grants, and license plate fees, such as the manatee and sea turtle plates seen on many Florida cars. Founded in 1956 as the Florida Marine Research Institute it was merged in 2004, along with two other state agencies, to become the FWRI. It provides " . . . the scientific foundation for Florida's fish and wildlife resources."[62] FWRI's emphasis is on collaboration with other scientific non-profit enterprises, stakeholders, academic institutions and government agencies both state and federal, working on fisheries and wildlife research in Florida. The state legislature had already funded the Florida Marine Research Institute laboratory and other facilities, completed, in 1994, for $10 million, and were relying upon the FWRI to gather statistical data to help in analyzing seasonal patterns and duration of red tide blooms. While the current data base goes back to 1878, many of the entries up to 1998 are questionable. First, they are sourced from anecdotal reports by fishermen and individuals, with little scientific background. Secondly, the duration and geographic extent of blooms was observational, captured after an event was recognized and identified while limited by the observer's mobility. And third, varying sampling techniques added to the uncertainty of original source information. In addition, many blooms were initiated, and transported at varying water column levels, beneath the surface of the Gulf where observers would be unable to detect the progress and extent of a bloom. Bearing in mind these shortcomings, the record is nonetheless revealing.

In the early years, up until the eighteen-month outbreak in 1993—1995, there was a strong sense that blooms were generally short-lived and that dissipation depended, in part, on cooler weather and northwest winds associated with late fall and winter cold fronts blowing through south Florida. That was borne out by the statistical evidence, despite being somewhat scanty and created from anecdotal reports

For example, during the one hundred seventeen years, from 1878 through 1994, only eight outbreaks took place in January and February. Only three of those, 1947, 1955 and 1982 lasted more than two months. However, in the twenty-four years, from 1995 to 2018, there were seventeen outbreaks in January and February, thirteen of which lasted for more than two months.

Perhaps the most startling number of all: from 1878 to August 1994, there were sixty-four months, in which red tide was present.[63] Comparing that to the period September 1994 through December 2018, red tide covered some part of the Florida coastal landscape for one hundred eighty-four months, so, during the three hundred four months, red tide was present for over 60% of the time.

In terms of duration, while the 1953—1955 bloom spanned a full eighteen months, from September through February, it was eclipsed by a thirty-month event from September 1994, until it finally dissipated in February 1997. This indicated a major shift in the duration of outbreaks and it was the prolonged presence of red tide beginning in 1994, combined with fresh water cyanobacteria originating in Lake Okeechobee, that finally brought both focus and sustained attention from both the state and federal government, in order to regularly fund previously sputtering research efforts. This vigorous new commitment produced a scattering of studies, task forces and legislation.

Clearly, something had changed in the Gulf as well as in Washington and Tallahassee. It was either an unlikely alteration to the chemistry of *K. brevis* that caused the blooms to survive the diminished hours, lower angle of winter sunlight and cooler water of winter accompanied by stronger winds, or an increase in anthropogenic sources like urban runoff, fertilizers and leaking septic tanks feeding releases into coastal waters and near shore estuaries.

Long-term human health studies begin

Woods Hole Oceanographic Institution was founded in 1930, in Falmouth, Massachusetts, following establishment of the Marine Biological Laboratory in 1888. During its illustrious years as one of the world's leading non-profit research bodies studying ocean habitat, it has attracted fifty-eight Nobel Prize winners. Today, much of the salt-water study is affiliated with the University of Chicago as the Marine Biological Laboratory, while other parts of the organization deal with science-based solutions to worldwide environmental issues like climate change.

While human health had been the subject of some research projects, illnesses from eating toxic fish, oysters and mussels was spreading from Maine to Oregon. This stimulated concern about the nation's aquatic food supply, both fish and shellfish, and Woods Hole decided to deal with the issue on a national scale.

In 1993, funded by the NOAA Coastal Oceans Program and National Marine Fisheries Service, Woods Hole convened a panel of twenty-four experts, for four days, to create a national plan that would deal with marine biotoxins from harmful algae blooms. The panel identified four general areas with human illness as directly caused by toxic algal blooms: paralytic, neurotoxic, diarrheic, and amnesic shellfish poisoning. The first three were all caused by dinoflagellates such as *K. brevis*, and the last by diatoms, little single-celled microalgae roaming the world's oceans and producing oxygen as a byproduct of photosynthesis.

They were previously thought to be harmless to humans, but that was changing.

The underlying message from the panel was that while the United States had experienced sporadic blooms of algal cells regionally, since the early 1970s, every coastal state and some inland waters like Lake Erie, were now threatened by one or more different species capable of doing damage to the food supply, the environment, the local economy and human health. Eutrophication of estuaries, climate change and aquaculture operations leading to highly localized concentrations of enriched nutrients all contributed to the growing problem, while increased monitoring and oversight of coastal waters led to greater awareness.

After reviewing the body of scientific studies already available, the Woods Hole panel was convinced that the biggest deficiency was a lack of coordination and consolidation of evidence leading to the creation of an overall picture. Blame was placed entirely on government. "No federal agency has assumed a leadership role in coordinating and supporting the studies needed to optimize management and mitigation strategies. Research funding has always been sporadic and limited."[64] More specifically, no acceptable consistent and uniform standards for toxins were made widely available, methods for assaying by vessel and in the laboratory were lacking, and field sampling programs in existence at the time were inadequate, for detecting and describing the extent and intensity of the blooms.

The report was quietly absorbed into the bureaucracy but would soon form the basis for a major federal undertaking—the ECOHAB project of 1994—which would emerge as the main focal point for gathering papers, studies and results of scientific inquiry, through the turn of the century and well beyond.

1994-1997 outbreak

The bloom was detected on September 16, 1994, in both Charlotte Harbor and the Gulf of Mexico. Mote Marine staff and vessels were in the area at the time and able to begin sampling off the coast at Sarasota three days after the bloom first appeared. Four days later the concentration, based on samples in the Gulf, exceeded twelve million per liter and in Charlotte Harbor reached twenty-three million per liter versus a general background of 1,000 cells per liter. The numbers in the Gulf remained high, exceeding six million, until around October 1st when the concentrations dropped. But, closer to the coast and land-based nutrients, the outbreak had moved to Longboat Key and by early November, the count at Sands Point on the Gulf side was the astonishing number of over sixty-eight million cells per liter.

By the end of October, things started to quiet down. Red tide in Sarasota Bay never reached the intensity of the outbreak in the Gulf, causing Mote Marine scientists to conclude that the combination of conditions in the Bay must have been altered in some way.[65] The Mote report was filed in June 1995, but in January 1996, the red tide bloom returned with a vengeance, this time spreading all the way from Sarasota Bay down to the Florida Keys.

The how and why this happened became uppermost in the public's mind as the bloom decimated the local manatee population of south Florida and had a dramatic effect on all aquatic life in the rivers and estuaries, feeding into the eastern Gulf. The 1994-1997 bloom killed two hundred thirty-eight manatees, almost all of them in 1996 and 1997. It was the longest and most devastating outbreak in south Florida's history.

Manatee mortality

The East Indian manatee is a large, aquatic mammal; a vegetarian similar, in many ways, to its bovine counterpart on land. These gentle giants of the Gulf can grow to four meters in length and weigh up to 600 kilograms—over a half ton. Moving slowly, using their front flippers for propulsion and steering, they graze on both fresh and salt-water plants, ranging from delectable water lettuce to the more bitter mangrove leaves, consuming anywhere from 10-15% of their body weight daily. This is accomplished by spending almost one-third of their day munching on the abundant grasses of the Gulf and its rivers and estuaries. They have four rows of teeth which are being constantly replaced, as they are worn down by the grinding motion and grit from their diet. They are able to manipulate their lips while using front flippers to direct food into their mouth where they masticate using a series of muscles and horned ridges along the jaw line.

As vegetarians, manatees would not ingest enough red tide from their sea grass diet alone to be fatal, but necropsy of a small number showed that death was due to a disruption of the nervous system. Further study, by the Florida Marine Patrol and scientists at the University of Miami, showed that the culprits were sea squirts, or ascidians. As filter feeders, sea squirts bioaccumulated large amounts of neurotoxins while attaching themselves to the sea grasses, on which manatees fed.

In order to survive, the West Indian manatee needs water that exceeds 15° Celsius, because of their low metabolic rate. It has always been difficult to get an accurate count of Florida's total manatee population but according to the U. S. Fish and Wildlife Service it was estimated at 2,639, in the winter of 1996. By January 1997, the count had dropped to 2,229 and the next month to 1,706. Estimates were done during cold weather months because manatees tended to congregate near warm water sources, such as power plant outflows, and the extraordinary population loss was partly due to the presence of algal blooms and resulting lack of dissolved oxygen.[66]

According to the Florida Fish and Wildlife Conservation Commission, 166 of the gentle sea cows died as a direct consequence of red tide during 1996-1997, and another 210 from "other" causes undetermined.[67] The numbers, adding toxic induced mortality and "other" causes didn't add up. The drop in the population was written off as a possible error from the airborne census, which was notoriously unreliable, because only manatees visible close to the surface of the area surveyed could be seen and others might have been stacked like cord wood.

This was the opinion of Kathy Cookman, owner and guide of Manatee Eco & River Cruises in Fort Meyers. "I just don't trust those counts. They are supposed to be done at the same time of year, but that's not always the case. And, there are so many variables like water temperature that affect the population. If it's warm they will move out to the Gulf, away from the areas where they do the counts. It's not reliable."[68]

Feds enter the picture

The first meaningful federal initiative had occurred, in 1993, when seven (later twelve) agencies joined, with the Seminole and Miccosukee tribes and five state and local government entities, to form the South Florida Ecosystem Restoration Task Force (SFERTF), at the request of the Secretary of the Interior, Bruce Babbitt, a committed environmental advocate. Funded within the department, among the stated goals were two critically important elements: to facilitate interagency and intergovernmental agreement about restoration, and to coordinate and avoid duplication in scientific research. An allied Working Group was later expanded to twenty-five members with connections to south Florida, tasked with coordinating development and prioritization of programs, strategies and on-the-ground projects to facilitate restoration.

SFERTF was later funded, by Congressional appropriation, through the Water Resources Development Act (WRDA), of 1996, and deepened federal involvement by requiring the Corps, through a program called the Restudy, to find hydrologic solutions to restore the south Florida ecosystem. The Corps had been responsible for designing and building the C&SF project and was the go-to government agency, for timing of water discharges from Lake Okeechobee. The Restudy was the first crack at addressing restoration across multiple government agencies, tribal interests, agricultural, environmental and urban needs. Buoyed by the results, in the 2000 WRDA bill, the Congress authorized implementation of many Restudy recommendations, titling it the Comprehensive Everglades Restoration Plan, better known by its acronym CERP.

The 2000 bill creating CERP was signed by President George W. Bush, with much hoopla, on the same day the U. S. Supreme Court was hearing one of its landmark cases titled *Bush vs. Gore*. It was a chance for federal and state governments to show that they were serious about restoration of the hydrologic pieces of the south Florida ecosystem, and to back up the many promises lightly made in thousands of pages of reports and recommendations. It was the opportunity of a lifetime that would eventually drag itself to a ragged conclusion, of partial funding, lackadaisical regulation and bureaucratic inertia that exist to this day.

ECOHAB

Two years before CERP, and following the massive 1994-1997 outbreak, Congress passed the Harmful Algal Bloom and Hypoxia Research and Control Act of 1998. This was the first attempt to provide sustained federal funding, appropriated annually, to study the dimensions of the growing national problem of harmful algae bloom outbreaks from the Oregon coast to the Florida Keys.

Dubbed as ECOHAB by Donald Anderson, a senior scientist at Woods Hole and director of the Coastal Ocean Institute, the project design came out of a series of UNESCO sponsored programs, to prepare less developed countries for the effects of algal blooms. Anderson became interested in the subject while a graduate student at MIT when a massive outbreak occurred along the Massachusetts coast, and he decided to devote his illustrious career to studying the cellular origins and molecular structure of toxin genetics. And in his spare time, he managed to become the Massachusetts Amateur Senior golf champion.

The goal of the United States' ECOHAB program was "... to develop an understanding of the population stated dynamics and trophic impacts of harmful algal species which can be used as a basis for minimizing adverse effects on the economy, public health, and marine ecosystems."[69] Funding was generous, growing from $15 million, in 1999, to $19 million, in 2001.

The most important idea behind the undertaking was to have a single focal point from which interagency governmental efforts and private researchers could be coordinated into directed research to develop a national strategy to deal with the problem. State agencies were invited to join in by designing initiatives appropriate to their needs, and ECOHAB Florida was one of the first to jump in. As examples, the FWRI was given a grant in October 1998, of $975,000 to study origination and stimulation of red tides, and the Florida Fish and Wildlife Conservation Commission a $450,000 grant, in 2001, to study the transport of red tide from the WFS to the coast.

In December 2000, while the ink was still drying on the WRDA bill, Woods Hole convened a meeting of Florida investigators, twenty-three at the time, representing thirteen different institutions and agencies, to discuss the status of their projects. This was exactly the purpose of ECOHAB. In 2004, Congress reauthorized the act, with annual appropriations starting at $23.5 million annually and expanding it to $25.5 million, to cover fresh water outbreaks partially in response to the disaster created by Florida's rivers emptying into Tampa Bay and Charlotte Harbor.

The federal government has maintained its support of the program through 2018, at a level slightly above $20 million, based upon the assumption that the majority of underlying science had been completed and attention should be turned to methods of controlling outbreaks.

Over the more than two decades of its existence, ECOHAB funded dozens of researchers in Florida institutions, ranging from universities to state agencies, all contributing to the vast and growing body of knowledge of the life cycle of algae blooms along the Florida coast.

State of Florida's sputtering start

The Restudy, from the federal side that stimulated Congressional action in 2000, had begun in 1996, funded partly by NOAA, and was first completed and made public in January 1999. While many of the recommendations dealt with the quantity and distribution of surface water, the section on water quality pointed out that the Everglades and coastal estuaries had been seriously degraded by man-made pollutants.

"Water quality conditions in Lake Okeechobee are not likely to significantly improve unless substantial lake inflow pollution load reductions occur, and action is taken to reduce in-lake nutrient levels. The Restudy should emphasize restoration of the Lake Okeechobee ecosystem, including its water quality." [70]

For the first time, legacy phosphorous, hardened into a layer of muck at the bottom of the lake, was identified as an impediment to cleaning up the water, as was the polluted sediment from animal waste in the Kissimmee River feeding in from the north. The report admitted that the lake was eutrophic and even if modifications were made to nutrient content of the inflows, it would have little effect, because of the legacy phosphorous, hence, the idea of dredging the bottom of a 730 sq. mi. lake and restore the original, sandy bottom. It was set out, without regard to a reliable estimate of the volume or how to dispose of the residue.

The real problem was that the recommendations, so urgently put, reflected a light touch when it came to regulation. For example, while urging that urban and agricultural runoff "... assure that water from non-natural sources (e.g. urban, industrial and agricultural sources) meet all water quality performance measures that are designed for restoration of the natural system before being discharged to the natural system," the state's solution was to encourage Best Management Practices (BMPs) without sanctions.[71] The obvious weakness was that, if a farmer signed an agreement to institute BMPs, it was automatically considered a "presumption of compliance" whether anything was ever done or not.

The state had already found, in 1986, that requiring dairy farmers to maintain offal on their property had a beneficial effect on the Kissimmee River drainage, but the task force had gingerly walked away from further regulation, in favor of voluntary action which, as time went on, would satisfy corporate agricultural interests and municipalities not wanting to spend money to replace or upgrade water and waste treatment facilities, but did nothing to improve water quality.

There is an important point here, and that is the Corps of Engineers is not responsible for water quality. Their charge has always been to manage the navigable waterways of the United States, regardless of the chemical content of the rivers they manage. That's not to say the employees and contractors of the Corps are indifferent to water quality. They are not. But it was put well by Lt. Col. Jennifer Reynolds, in 2019.

"Priorities change. When the Corps is asked by the state to create opportunities for agriculture, it goes to work and does a good job. When the priorities shift, and the Corps is asked to mitigate the Kissimmee, from a virtual canal into a meandering river with oxbows and areas where excess water can spread out, we will do a good job. When it comes to water quality, that is not something we can do much about despite the fact that we, as human beings, don't sometimes like to see the aftereffects of what we are tasked to do." [72]

Florida Legislature chimes in

With ECOHAB formed at the federal level, the state of Florida embarked on three different paths, some converging and some colliding. The first was an advisory board that was formed and reported directly to Governor Lawton Chiles. The second, coming three years later, was a group established by the then Secretary of State (and a Chiles appointee) Virginia Wetherell. We shall discuss these two groups in detail, as an example of the difficulties the State of Florida encountered in dealing with the political baggage that always accompanied environmental issues.

A third group, following on the heels of ECOHAB, and in reaction to public pressure, after the 1994–1997 outbreak, was created, in 1999 by the state legislature as an advisory board to study the origins and effects of red tide. The enabling statute, which remains on the books to this day, states that the purpose of the working group was "...determining research, monitoring, control, and mitigation strategies for red tide and other harmful algal blooms in Florida waters."[73]

Members would be appointed and report their findings and recommendations back to the Fish and Wildlife Research Institute (FWRI), part of the Florida Fish and Wildlife Conservation Commission at the time. The program was lightly funded and sputtered along for two years, until 2001, when it was defunded by act of the legislature, by specifying the per cent allocation of license fees for multiple purposes, and by squeezing the available funds for marine research projects, effectively discontinuing underwriting of the task force. The task force did continue to meet, and file reports with the FWRI, but it never reached the level of importance for which it was intended.

Jeb Bush was governor at the time. He had good environmental chops, but by 2001 the memory of the 1994–1997 outbreaks had faded and other priorities, such as increasing the number of public boat launch facilities, occupied the political wizards in Tallahassee. This pattern would be repeated, in Florida time after time, as political priorities tended more to immediate needs and less to long-term solutions, particularly ones with vast differences of opinion as to methods and outcomes, as was the case with restoration of south Florida's disintegrating ecosystem.

2005-2006 outbreak

A bloom began off the southwestern coast of Florida, in January 2005. First detected by satellite twenty miles west of St. Petersburg, it followed record rainfall in 2004, due to a series of hurricanes—Charley, Frances, Ivan and Jeanne. The Corps of Engineers, fearing a breach of the Hoover Dike, began water releases from Lake Okeechobee down the Caloosahatchee River, beginning in the fall of 2004 and throughout almost all of 2005, in both wet seasons and dry. The massive *K. brevis* bloom that developed led to hypoxic zones offshore and in Charlotte Harbor, Tampa Bay and Sarasota Bay, as it moved from the Gulf into the near shore regions, causing the die-off of hundreds of sea turtles, ninety-three manatees, birds and uncountable other creatures living in the benthic habitat of the coastal waters. The bloom would last for thirteen months, fed by nutrient releases down the Caloosahatchee and further fueled by die-off pockets of nitrogen (N) released as ammonium (NH_4+), in "dead zones," hastening the process of decomposition of organic matter.

The bloom moved predictably north, and at its peak, in January 2005, created a dead zone of nearly 2,000 square miles, three to twenty-three miles offshore, stretching from New Port Richey to Sarasota. Mortality off Tampa Bay was the result of low dissolved oxygen and brevetoxins, creating a mass of dead and dying organic material that settled to the bottom. In the period from June to September 2005, Sarasota scraped up 1.5 million pounds of dead aquatic creatures from its beaches.

In July 2005, with a weak El Niño, Saharan dust, with heavy rainfall, blew across the Atlantic and summer thunderstorms moving west, from the Everglades to the coast, dumped it into the Gulf of Mexico, stimulating *Trichodesmium* cells to a growth phase that accelerated the existing *K. brevis* bloom to even higher levels. By the late summer, the bloom extended, from the coast of Alabama to the Florida Keys, covering 8,000 sq. miles.

"This Red Tide is stronger than anything I have ever seen before," said Sarasota boat captain Wayne Genthner, who remembers 2005 well. "It seems to be killing quicker."[74] Genthner's business dropped by 85% as a result of the red tide outbreak. There were other reports of divers' silver jewelry turning black from low dissolved oxygen, and a smell akin to that of rotten eggs.

Hurricane Katrina blew through the area, in August, but despite stirring up the water column and increasing oxygen levels, failed to have an immediate impact on the red tide, which gradually dissipated by February 2006.

The 2005-2006 bloom stimulated an outpouring of scientific studies and papers, some of which confirmed elements of the developing standard *K. brevis* bloom model while others were either clearly contradictory or brought to light additional information, adding to the rapidly growing body of knowledge of phytoplankton appearing with regularity off Florida's west coast.

Questioning the Saharan dust theory

In a classic scientific confrontation, a direct question, as to whether Saharan dust deposition had any effect upon the initiation cycle of K. brevis, was introduced by a team from the University of South Florida. The U. S. Geological Survey hypothesized that submarine groundwater discharges, mainly from Florida's iconic springs in the central part of the state, abetted by septic tank leakage, was the primary stimulus for maintaining the 2005–2006 bloom off the coast, pointing out that the year was marked by a weak summer El Niño Southern Oscillation, which promoted Atlantic hurricane development, but that evidence of Saharan dust deposition was lacking.[75]

The El Niño phenomenon is a band of warming water, in the equatorial Pacific Ocean. The normal interval between events is two to five years, and the warming takes place, for around seven to nine months. It waxes and wanes between cold and warm and changes the wind shear of the Lower Pacific Jet Stream that crosses the North American continent, peaking during the winter months. At the upper levels of the atmosphere, the easterly flow (from Florida to Africa) is strengthened while at lower levels the westerly flow is slightly favored. Tropical cyclones are not vertically aligned, with the storm tops blowing eastward, as the lower levels move toward the west off the coast of Africa. If the El Niño weakens, during the Atlantic hurricane season, as it did it 2004 and 2005, the cyclonic storms remain vertically aligned, as the trade winds move them from the cost of African toward North America.

Weather data showed that precipitation, during the summer of 2004, was extremely high, well past normal levels, draining discharges into the west coast rivers feeding the Gulf, into 2005. They pointed out that the possibility of groundwater creating a low nitrogen environment needed further study as an alternative to the Saharan dust theory.

The science coming into the peer review grinder at the time was challenging and sometimes contradictory to conventional thinking. In one way, it was a healthy development, because the more known about nutrient sources the more likely action would be taken to either mitigate or eliminate the root cause of the problem. Cutting another way, it offered state political and regulatory agencies a reason for dithering over intervening, based upon the argument that the science was unsettled, and until some broad consensus was reached, any actions taken could have unintended consequences. But not all science challenged conventional wisdom; some broke entirely new ground and a good example was a study of the relationship between nutrient location and phytoplankton venue.

Different locations mean different blooms

The West Florida Shelf area is fed by three major rivers: the Peace feeding into northern Charlotte Harbor, the Caloosahatchee coming into central and southern Charlotte Harbor and the Shark River which, along which a number of smaller streams and drainages, works its way into Everglades National Park and eventually Florida Bay.

In a study published in 2007, scientists surveyed the WFS for nutrient levels, examining the ratio of nitrogen to phosphorous, during the dry season in 2003, set against concentrations of various phytoplankton. What they found was that "... terrestrial nutrient inputs are large, even during minimal flow, and that their relative availability leads to both differential nutrient limitation in different regions of the shelf as well as development of a varying plankton community composition." [76]

They concluded that dinoflagellates' primary zone for bloom maintenance was near the coast, in a long, narrow, longitudinal strip from Tampa Bay to just north of Naples, fed mainly by Peace River nutrients coming from citrus, diary and phosphate from both natural washing of surficial deposits and mining operations. A second zone, beginning out beyond the dinoflagellate zone in the Gulf and stretching down to Flamingo and Everglades National Park, in the shape of a tear drop, had higher concentrations of cyanobacteria, from agricultural and legacy phosphorous, sent down the Caloosahatchee River. The third zone, starting even further west out beyond

Charlotte Harbor, went all the way down into Florida Bay past Key West.

The important distinction made by the study was in the balance between nitrogen and phosphorous, the N: P ratio of particulate matter (as opposed to dissolved chemicals), in each of the three zones. The first zone was nitrogen limited, the second balanced and third phosphorous limited. It had been confirmed, by other studies, that that dinoflagellates thrived as the N: P ratio declined and that while inorganic nutrients might be low, *Trichodesmium*, once activated in the vicinity, had the ability to "fix" and make available organic nitrogen and other chemicals sufficient to encourage and maintain *K. brevis* blooms.

In the second zone, the presence of urea was presumed to be a major source of nitrogen for cyanobacteria. It had been increasing dramatically in lawn fertilizers, with worldwide use having increased one-hundred-fold, since 1950.

And in the third area, the prevalent algae were diatoms, microscopic unicellular algae with transparent silica cell walls. Under a microscope, they look like a Petri dish and in high concentrations with warming water as a stimulus, can become "brown tide," but also reflect light as green in color. Photosynthetic and common to all water bodies, fresh and salt, there are about 16,000 species worldwide; they provide nearly half the production of organic material in the oceans. They reproduce by cell division in a boom-bust cycle, with the boom beginning as water warms.

In shallow Florida Bay, with abundant sea grasses, the

high biomass can smother grasses and sponges that benthic species use for food. In 1994, the ecosystem collapsed due to high nutrient runoff, from the Everglades Agricultural Area south of Lake Okeechobee. The cause of the collapse was heavily debated—from the cutoff of fresh water to Everglades National Park to increased nitrogen from urea-laden fertilizer—and led to the Everglades Forever Act of 1995, requiring cane sugar growers to pay over $300 million to clean up their fields.

Dueling scientists

The FWRI data base produced fuel for another study. In an attempt to pin down the causes of increased activity and biomass of *K. brevis* blooms along the coast, Larry Brand and Angela Compton of the Rosenstiel School did a statistical analysis of blooms, concluding that within five kilometers of the coast, they were twenty-times more abundant than at twenty to thirty kilometers offshore, and "13-18-fold more abundant in 1994-2002 than in 1954-1963."[77]

Brand was one of the titans of research on red tide. Professor of Marine Biology and Fisheries at the University of Miami, he had trained at MIT and Woods Hole Oceanographic Institute. His early work focused on dinoflagellates and cyanobacteria, until he moved on to studies showing the long-term effects on human health of blue-green algae eruptions—covered in the next chapter of this book. He and Compton had co-authored a number of studies over the years, combining their efforts to bring attention to the subject of human health as a result of HABs.

Using data from the FWRI files, they concluded that a seasonal shift took place between the two comparative periods of 1954–1963 and 1994–2002, being few and far between in the spring and summer of the earlier period, picking up in October through January and then abating in the spring. In the second period studied, blooms tended to start earlier, in August, and last in heavy concentrations through the late winter and spring, the time when most tourists visited south Florida.

Brand and Compton then set out a new line of argument: that the initiation phase of a bloom cycle was not necessarily the result of an external event like the deposit of Saharan dust, but rather the result of years of buildup of nutrients in the WFS from land-based runoff residing in sediment, sea grasses and other forms of long-lasting deposits.

"We hypothesize that this large reservoir of nutrients on the West Florida Shelf ultimately allows for the development of blooms with nutrient requirements that exceed the actual input of nutrients at any given time. This could explain why estimates of nutrients from river flow alone (Vargo et al., 2004; Hu et al., 2006) appear to sometimes be insufficient to support some of the largest blooms. It is hypothesized that processes currently not understood allow for the eventual transfer of nutrients from these benthic pools to *K. brevis* under certain circumstances, promoting its increase in biomass." [78]

The argument continues by asserting that once the bloom moves onshore, land-based nutrients boost the concentrations to significantly higher levels based on a series of samples in coastal estuaries.

This was a difficult approach because it placed blame squarely on point and non-point (but generally known) sources that exercised political muscle in Tallahassee and Washington. Admitting that the mechanisms involved in the initiation phase were still an unsettled question, the assertion was clear. "Sampling bias, long-term changes or oscillations in the ecosystem, increases in iron-stimulated nitrogen fixation,"[79] all may contribute to the increase extent and coverage of blooms, the blame was placed squarely on human activities such as agriculture, fertilizers, and leaking septic tanks, all of which contributed over time to the pollution of the ecosystem well beyond near shore coastal waters.

Political fault lines enter the picture

Following closely on the heels of the Brand and Compton study, Mote Marine issued its own white paper, filled with cautious nostrums. In a typical academic imbroglio, Mote scientists dismissed the validity of the hypothesis that land-based effluent was the main cause of red tide blooms. Citing the inherent inconsistency of sampling techniques included in the FWRI data base as a viable basis for statistical analysis, Mote emphasized the political nature of the debate, following the historical 2005–2006 outbreak. "The science of Florida red tide is complex, and strongly held viewpoints have contributed to the politicization of scientific debates,"[80] an open admission that the issue extended into the halls of the capital at Tallahassee.

The main author was Frank Alcock, who had been named director of the Marine Policy Institute at its founding, in 2006. Mote was a venerable institution, one of Florida's full-service, non-profit, research institutions. First opened, in 1955, and based in Sarasota as the Cape Haze Marine Laboratory, it changed its name, in honor of the Mote family for their financial support. Today, it employs over two hundred scientists, with a large aquarium at its campus on City Island in Sarasota Bay, and has been involved in ocean science research and restoration projects worldwide.

The Marine Policy Institute was created to for a more local focus with the specific purpose of producing credible science to give policy makers advice and counsel as to solutions for environmental issues confronting south Florida's booming economy and growing population. Its philosophy was, and continues to be to this day, expressed in cautious terms:

"It is imperative that scientists, policy makers and stakeholders move beyond polarized debate surrounding the links between coastal pollution and red tide. Conclusive scientific evidence of a strong linkage between coastal pollution and red tide blooms would no doubt generate political momentum for a pollution-reduction agenda. However, the nature of nutrient conditions on the West Florida Shelf and the variety of nutrient sources the likely contribute to red tides make it very difficult to pinpoint or assess the relative significance of each source. Conclusive evidence remains elusive, but Florida needs to act now. Florida needs to reduce nutrient loads to its watersheds for reasons that go beyond red tide and it needs to develop a comprehensive management strategy for red tides that goes beyond reducing coastal pollution." [81]

In this statement, the politics of red tide are artfully exposed. The fault lines, the interstices where strongly held opinions diverged, were left to speculation, but the message was clear. All the science to date, hundreds upon hundreds of academic peer-reviewed papers, consortia and presentations, had carefully skirted the political dynamic at work, but here finally was an institution committed to framing the discussion beyond the comfortable insularity of academia, and to bring it into the messy world of Florida politics.

The politics of deflection

The Mote Marine report, designed to offer policy makers science-based information, to aid in making decisions that were set forth but never openly broached, had a core problem: a lack of clear leadership as to what state agency had primary responsibility to make policy recommendations to the governor's office and legislature.

In an alphabet soup of acronyms, Mote identified six federal agencies, five state agencies and five local and regional groups, all of which had differing degrees and areas of responsibility for water management in the State of Florida.[82]

And while the scientists worked through the back and forth, with peer review of specialized research, it gave cover to government agencies in deciding how to organize an effort to stem the growing problem, until a glimmer of light appeared in the form of a report, in September 2008, that stirred Congress to action.

National response plan—HAB report

The Interagency Task Force, formed by the Harmful Algae Bloom and Hypoxia Act of 2004, offered a series of reports to Congress, in 2007 and 2008. Well received, it was followed by enabling legislation stipulating that the group should report back in five different areas.[83]

In its report dated August 2008, the Task Force, representing the coordinated efforts of a laundry list of agencies ranging from the National Aeronautics and Space Administration (NASA) to the U. S. Fish and Wildlife Service (USFWS), laid out federal plans for dealing with the growing national problem, while admitting up front that twenty-five states were doing their own, independent planning, because the vast majority of blooms occurred within state waters, as was the case in Florida.

Titled Harmful Algae Blooms Management and Response: Assessment and Plans, what was submitted to the Congress is instructive, in both what it contains and what it does not. The areas selected for further study were (1) monitoring, (2) prediction, (3) control, (4) event response, (5) coordination, (6) incentive-based programs to improve prediction and response, and (7) economic and sociocultural impacts.

The federal emphasis was clearly on monitoring, prediction, control, event response and coordination among federal and state agencies. Statements like: "HABs are a natural phenomenon in coastal ecosystems, but human activities are thought to increase the frequency of HABs. For example, although not all HABs occur in high nutrient environments, increased nutrient loading has been acknowledged as a likely factor contributing to the increased occurrence of high biomass HABs," or "...in those areas where HABs have been linked to nutrient pollution, possible preventive strategies could include controlling point and non-point source nutrient inputs and modifying land use practices"[84] amounted to little more than dancing around the real issue—control and mitigation of point and non-point source nutrients entering and unbalancing coastal ecosystems throughout the United States. The one word that is conspicuously sparse and appears in the document only twice is "prevention."

In effect, the Interagency group was walking a fine line on point and nonpoint sources, by putting the nexus of research and causality on outside research without making a serious commitment to opening up the discussion about what those sources might be and how to prevent them from doing further damage. The controlling factor was a disclaimer: "Only proactive measures of prevention that apply to current knowledge are considered in this report."[85] But the disclaimer ignored hundreds of papers, backed by thousands of hours of research, which placed blame squarely on three factors, urban runoff and the use of lawn fertilizers, agriculture including crop, dairy and cattle, and leaking septic tanks.

In a more favorable interpretation, the report brought to light the need to share external studies that might relate to issues in other states and regions. For example, the City of Wichita, Kansas, had developed a state-of-the-art, continuous system for monitoring water coming from its local reservoir for *geosmin*, a cyanobacteria compound that federal guidelines said should not exceed 0.01 mg/liter. Information sharing was an advantage of having overall federal coordination of academic studies, as in ECOHAB, sharing on-the-ground anecdotes from various parts of the country. Sixteen federal funding programs were involved in the overall effort, as well as twenty intramural programs studying methods to predict and respond to blooms. It also gave state and local regulatory authorities an inventory of successful, and unsuccessful, means of managing outbreaks once they occurred, to prevent duplicating the mistakes of others.

To its credit, the task force placed human health issues at the forefront of its report, as the most significant impact of HABs, even beyond commercial and monetary considerations to local economies.

At the top of the list: "Cyanobacteria are the major, harmful, algal group in freshwater environments; their toxins ('cyanotoxins') are a potential threat for drinking water supplies."[86] Next came the salt water algae: "In Florida, beachgoers and people working or living near the water can be exposed via sea spray aerosols, to neurotoxins produced by the species *K. brevis*, resulting in respiratory irritation in healthy people and potentially debilitating acute events in people with underlying respiratory illnesses such as asthma."[87]

By implementing elements of the proposed plan, the working group believed it could mitigate human health impacts while minimizing economic disruption. All well and good, but there was only one mention of preventing the rapidly increasing incidence of and coverage of algal blooms throughout the United States.

The report goes on to state tentatively that "... it is generally accepted that some HAB events are intensified by high nutrients."[88] It goes on to assert that the agencies responsible would be EPA and the U. S. Department of Agriculture (USDA), a tacit admission that the sources of nutrient runoff, both point and some non-point, were well known. But the report goes no further. It stands as passive acceptance that little can be done to prevent outbreaks, without having a dramatic effect upon government agencies, sewer districts and communities in coastal watersheds. This was unfortunate, because almost all the pressure to create standards for cyanotoxins was the responsibility of the federal government and very little on the states.

The important element in the report should not be overlooked. It is that human health issues were coming to the forefront of both scientific inquiry and the public mind. They would broadly increase over time as new research, and new measurement techniques became available, and would be heavily debated as befits all health issues. This is covered in the next chapter.

CHAPTER 7

Harmful Algal Blooms and Human Health

◆———·•◆•·——◆

As awareness that red tide was a growing problem, both temporally and spatially, the scientific community turned its attention to the effects on human health, and to provide some context, it's instructive to go back in time to when human health first became a concern, albeit minor, of the state and federal governments.

Early anecdotal evidence back into the 19th century is quite thin and tangentially suggested that respiratory irritation might be a problem, along with consumption of shellfish from bloom-affected areas but in 1917, with a letter written by George Skermer Harden Taylor of the Bureau of Fisheries was able to document first-hand evidence of human distress.

"The early morning of [October 3rd] the Gulf was covered with these fish as far as the eye could see. Soon after this drift commenced I went to the beach accompanied by a small dog; while on the beach I felt a slight tendency to sneeze and cough; shortly afterwards my attention was called to the action of the dog which was sneezing violently and seemed to be in acute distress, choking and showing every symptom of asphyxiation. I carried him off the beach and in a short time he seemed to recover, so I carried him back and the same thing happened again. I then noticed that my lungs were feeling sore and that my breathing was labored, in much the same manner as when I board ships after fumigation, except that I could notice no odor. Other people were affected the same way."[89]

George Skermer at the time was deputy tax collector of customs at Boca Grande guarding the north side of the entrance to Charlotte Harbor and regarded as a credible witness. He also wrote that he had contacted a number of fishing boat captains, finding that the same respiratory symptoms had affected them all, and most of their crews, when passing through bloom areas.

He then noted that on October 18th another bout of red tide moved in:

". . . (t)he gas was very violent this time and many people telephoned for medical assistance for 'cold in the head' "sore throats' 'cold in the chest' etc. besides coming to see the local physician, who is also the United States; quarantine surgeon here. I, myself, have suffered quite acutely for the past five days, but the worst of the gas seems to be going now." [90]

Although incidental to the main purpose of Taylor's report, which had as its focus fish and shellfish mortality, this was the first well-documented (although somewhat anecdotal) report of respiratory distress experienced by humans encountering red tide.

Skermer followed up with other letters describing fish kills, setting forth three important facts in his observations: first, that the water was discolored and generally dark and mainly red, second, that aerosolized *K. brevis* was odorless and third, that other mammals i.e. his "small dog" expressed similar symptoms. The last point was particularly relevant as much of the research done fifty years later scientists would use canines to test reactions to increasing levels of toxicity to aerosolized red tide.

However, the concern over human reactions was muted, primarily because the respiratory symptoms were temporary, inconvenient and did not affect everyone. But eating poisoned fish and shellfish was a different matter, although many of the causes of toxic effects were not medically proven until the late 1940s.

NSP

There are five different types of fish and shellfish poisoning worldwide, but we will concentrate on the one that is site-specific to coastal southwest Florida—neurotoxic shellfish poisoning (NSP) as a long term consequence of a red tide outbreak. It is a brevetoxin, part of a group of polyether compounds endemic to southwest Florida that have no odor or color which means that the normal warning signs of bad taste or smell are not present. Most important, NSP is heat stable which means that cooking will not damage or modify the chemistry, and eating contaminated fish tends to manifest itself as a digestive upset including nausea and diarrhea.

The Centers for Disease Control (CDC) of the U. S. Department of Health and Human Services parses NSP into three categories: food poisoning, infection and allergies. Of the possible sources shellfish (mussels, clams and oysters) are the most potent because they are filter feeders, sucking in large volumes of sea water to feed on suspended particles. Fish, on the other hand, take in the toxic water through their gills and die as a result, sometimes in less than five minutes depending upon the concentration and intensity of the bloom.

Today, the State of Florida does a good job of monitoring shellfish beds, but less is known about the effects of consuming fin fish impacted by brevetoxin. What is known is that hospital admissions for gastrointestinal problems in southwest Florida go up dramatically during red tide outbreaks and in some cases, as with Mrs. Hoy of Manatee County covered in chapter two, there could be vertigo and a lack of muscle coordination as well. It was clear to researchers that contact with the skin caused rashes. Neurotoxic poisoning takes effect from minutes up to three hours after eating contaminated shellfish. Recovery takes place over a period of days, but there is no evidence of permanent damage. Symptoms tend to be tingling in the feet and hands, nausea, diarrhea, and vertigo.

And, while diagnosis of the symptoms has always been straightforward, less is known about the pathology of the illness until recently when a number of studies have brought to light how brevetoxin interacts with the human digestive, respiratory and neurological systems much of which is covered later in this chapter.

Aerosolized red tide

Scientific interest on the effects of red tide on Florida residents and visitors tends today to be most concentrated during severe outbreaks, but arises from a period about thirty years ago when skepticism and caution reigned.

In addition, there were skeptics respected within the corridors of power. For example, in a 1964 paper produced for the Fish and Wildlife Service authors George Rounsefell and fellow researcher Walter Nelson took a very cautious tack. They were both eminent scientists at the University of Alabama, and their report was presented at a symposium sponsored by the Bureau of Commercial Fisheries, a subsidiary agency of the U. S. Department of the Interior. The report took anecdotal tales to task.

"The effect on the fish population has not been nearly as severe as the layman imagines when he hears of the death of millions of small fishes. The percentage kill is doubtless low. The kill of fishes by the 1946-1947 red tide was estimated by Gunter, Williams, Davis and Smith (1948) at 500 million fish. This figure may sound large, but actually it is not. If we realize that these fish will run no less than 10 to the pound, the total is only 50 million pounds. Every year about 1 billion pounds of menhaden are caught along a 300-mile stretch of the northern Gulf, but this enormous catch of a single species does not appear to be harming the supply." [91]

Further reading of the Rounsefell report offers another example of this tentative approach. "The effect of red tide on public health is rather debatable. For a short while during severe outbreaks there will be aerosols from breaking surf when the wind is blowing onshore .... A few people are so adversely affected that they must leave until the outbreak is over." [92]

This analysis was essentially correct in that when red tide cells rupture they release brevetoxins into both the air and the water, but this somewhat mushy write-up was significant because it came out in a widely circulated publication sponsored by the arm of the Federal government responsible for the economic well-being of the commercial fishing industry. It reviewed, and attempted to summarize, the findings of over 13,000 research papers in an attempt to synthesize the science to date, and was widely read. It's difficult to tell, given the source of funding, if the cautious tone was calculated to sooth or simply scientific skepticism.

However, the cautious approach began to lift when, in 1987, following five consecutive years of late summer and fall outbreaks an outpouring of studies relating to both respiratory and gastrointestinal problems flooded the scientific community studying red tide. A spate of papers issued in 1987 and 1988 had as a focus the effects on people with asthma who were dramatically affected by airborne red tide as a result of wind and surf breaking up the cells and releasing toxins into the air.

One early study by two physicians and a third researcher concluded that while people without underlying conditions felt immediate relief after leaving the beaches or entering air conditioning, 80% of asthmatics with hyper responsive airways experienced wheezing and airway constriction. Much of the evidence was obtained through studies on live canines and later on simulations of human reactions in a laboratory setting, but field studies on marine life impacted by red tide had been carried on for some time with interesting results. [93]

Mammal studies for brevetoxin effects

After the first major red tide event in 1982, 39 manatees died in Charlotte Harbor. In a necropsy conducted to find the medical causes of death, there was some evidence of brain lesions with a coincident red tide outbreak, but the study was not conclusive as to the exact source of the lesions.[94]

A decade later, after thorough investigation, a new set of studies from the Fish and Wildlife Conservation Commission was issued based upon the death of 149 manatees in Charlotte Harbor during the period March through May of 1996. Aerosolized brevetoxins were present during the outbreak, and the animals exhibited neuromuscular problems such as the inability to remain horizontal and back flexing. They also were afflicted by respiratory problems. In those autopsied there was a high level of brevetoxin in the brain, kidney, liver and stomach. Since the manatee diet consisted of seagrasses affected by the red tide, consumed up to 15% of their body weight daily, the path of brevetoxin through the organs made sense. But how it crossed the blood-brain barrier did not.

Later studies about cyanobacteria outbreaks would deal with this subject, but at the level of research in the mid-1990s, crossing the blood-brain barrier remained unexplained although one study done on lemon sharks asserted the connection between harmful algae blooms and neurochemical biomarkers positively.[95]

In another study, distressed but rescued manatees had blood samples taken and compared with a control group of unexposed and healthy specimens. The exposed group showed significantly lower lymphocyte counts when compared to the control group, leading to the conclusion that those manatees with a compromised immune system would probably suffer long-term health problems due to an inability to resist disease brought about by external influences.

While the effect of brevetoxin on manatee lymphoid tissue raises the question of a connection to human health in individuals exposed to aerosolized red tide over extended periods of time, the main point of the manatee studies was that mammals, like us, suffered significant tissue modification and organ damage, well beyond previously known respiratory discomfort. It set the stage for further studies on the longer term effects of red tide on human health. However, as a *caveat emptor,* none of the studies mentioned above related red tide outbreak symptoms directly to human beings. Correlation does not equal causality and a manatee, although a mammal like us, does not have the same body chemistry as we do.

County, state and federal information sources

Following the massive red tide outbreak in 1993 – 1995, and the one in 1996 so deadly to manatees, a sustained effort began on the part of health and regulatory authorities at all levels of government to create a timely notification system and to educate the public and tourists on the hazards of red tide. Early efforts included use of a telephone hotline operated by the Florida Poison Information Center in Miami. Callers were encouraged to report health problems, and the Center soon realized that there was a paucity of information about red tide and its effect on humans.

The Florida Department of Health, in conjunction with the Florida Fish and Wildlife Institute began to issue regular bulletins based upon weekly samples of areas suspected to have harmful algae blooms, particularly red tide, and advises the Department of Agriculture and Consumer Services responsible for closing areas to shell fishing of its sampling results. However, Florida monitors only oysters and clams, but not scallops. The muscle, the edible part of a scallop, does not bioaccumulate brevetoxin, and are less tolerant of red tide so die off quickly once exposed to the outbreak.

Federal interest was driven by the increasing coverage and extent of harmful algae blooms throughout the United States. The problem had become top of the mind in the 1960s when Lake Erie was declared to be "dead" and the connection with human health issues was delayed until the mid-1990s. More relevant, the federal interest was national, at a different level than local sourced information, so much of the data flowing from federal sources was background and reference to help state and local authorities illuminate and contextualize the issue.

Use of media

One of the best means of getting red tide information out to the public was the media in south Florida. In a study covering 1985 – 2012, the authors focused on how the risk factors were framed by local newspapers (radio and television were not covered in the study).[96]

The authors found that red tide was covered as and environmental story. Human health issues were dealt with extensively, mainly with anecdotal and human interest stories about people with respiratory problems and their concerns about the safety of seafood. There was very little written about public policy implications, partly born of a concern that the public might interpret some stories as a reason to change behavior by either not eating shellfish, or by changing their recreational patterns to the economic detriment of local businesses.

Not wanting to be perceived as morbidly negative, "... more than half the stories about blooms describe some form of intervention actions, especially research activities" which helped put a positive spin on the story.[97] And, there might have been a slight degree of self-interest as newspapers derived over 80% of their revenue from advertising, and had no desire to bite the hands that fed them with alarmist stories.

Impacts on human health by cyanobacteria—ancient prokaryotes

Much of the media and public information efforts by the State of Florida and local governments had red tide as the focus, but another threat to human health was coming from fresh water sources, mainly Lake Okeechobee, that would deserve attention—and that was cyanobacteria.

To prevent breaching of the 143-mile long Hoover Dike following on the heels of a damaging report from the U.S.

Army Corps of Engineers about the possible failure of the levee, the revised operating procedures brought a new threat to the estuaries of southwest Florida with periodic releases from the lake based upon keeping the water level at below 15.5 feet. Contained in those releases down the St. Lucie and Caloosahatchee Rivers was a new and highly toxic substance—cyanobacteria—formerly known as blue-green algae.

Cyanobacteria exists all over the world, from fresh water ponds and lakes to deserts where it comes blooming to life with seasonal rains. Scientists have classified it as an algae because it is capable of photosynthesis, but its origins are different from most other organisms classified as algae hence it was tagged as a bacteria.

Microbial life are the earliest forms of known life on the Earth, with cyanobacteria appearing about 3.5 billion years ago in the fossil record.[98] It was the planet's first photosynthesizer, using sunlight to make food and releasing oxygen as a byproduct of the process, helping to create what is known as the Great Oxidation Event, bringing new opportunities for life forms that eventually allowed human beings to populate the planet. As a byproduct, the introduction of oxygen in great quantities also set the stage for creation of inorganic iron (FE_2O_3) which helps us to date events reliably.

Some, but not all, cyanobacteria contains cyanotoxins, a powerful set of poisons, including one in particular—*microcystis aeruginosa*—believed to promote primary liver cancer in humans and another cyanobacterial toxin known as BMAA (β-N-methylamino-L-alanine) tied closely to neurodegenerative diseases like ALS (Lou Gehrig's disease), Alzheimer's and possibly Parkinson's. A study of one release from Lake Okeechobee turned up 30 different cyanotoxins with the preponderance being microcystins.[99]

Cyanobacteria are prokaryotes. Unlike *K. brevis*, but like other gram-negative bacteria lacks a well-defined nucleus, and the gelatinous cell wall, when exposed to salt water, begins to break down. The Gulf of Mexico has salinity of about 35 practical salinity units (PSU). Using dyes in a laboratory setting shows that the cell wall begins to break down at 18 PSU or about half the salinity of the Gulf. Moving to the real world, this would lead to the conclusion that as the cells are released down the Caloosahatchee River, they would begin to deteriorate west of the Franklin Lock and Dam, and release water soluble microcystins into the river where they have a half-life of about 4 to 14 days at the surface. But as dry scum, much like that seen in many canals in south Florida, it can last for as long as six months.[100]

Chronic exposure by human to cyanotoxins like *microcystis* at low levels of concentration comes mainly through the consumption of contaminated food such as fish, shrimp and prawns, direct exposure to the skin and by inhaling. The organ most directly impacted is the liver, but there is some evidence that the gastrointestinal tract and the kidneys can also be affected.[101] At higher levels, with an increase in biomass and concentration of cyanobacteria, drinking contaminated water can have a more dramatic effect. Studies also indicate that there may be a connection between ingestion of water infused with *microcystis* and colon cancer, but that is very preliminary and limited to one study.[102]

Microcystin—LR among the family of microcystins is highly toxic.[103] While primarily affecting the liver, it has been linked to cancer in humans and, while worldwide, has not been found in the fresh waters of south Florida so far.[104]

But the real questions are: how did we get to identify cyanobacteria as a possible cause of neurological disorders, and how does it insinuate into the human brain.

The answer to the first question involves a careful study of the history of scientific inquiry into BMAA. But the answer to the second question goes down two paths: the first by big pharmaceutical companies spending billions of dollars in hundreds of unsuccessful trials looking for a palliative for neurodegenerative diseases and the second a seemingly quixotic quest by one individual who surrounded himself with a world-wide consortium of scientists walking down an entirely different path of inquiry looking at BMAA.

Guam

To answer the first question, the story begins at the end of World War II on the island of Guam where American military doctors discovered that the indigenous people— the Chamorro—developed a disease they called lytico-bodig with many of the same symptoms as Parkinson's, Alzheimer's and ALS. Symptoms such as dementia and severe loss of motor skills including speech were observed in patients with lytico-bodig. The word is a combination from shortening the Spanish word "paralytico" and "bodig" is a native Chamorro word meaning listlessness.

At the peak of the disease, the Chamorro were one hundred times more likely to develop this disease than the rest of the world's population. Painstaking analysis of family trees disproved the earliest theory that the disease was genetic and was replaced by the theory that it was that a toxin in the cycad trees on Guam passed on through the seeds—which were thoroughly scrubbed before being ground into flour for tortillas. Later researchers argued that a Chamorro would have to eat one ton of cycad flour per month for the toxin to have any effect.

Guam soon became an epicenter for neurologists studying the pathology of neurodegenerative diseases in the hope that it might provide enough information to lead to better understand the origin of ALS and similar diseases. The cycad tree seeds were always in the crosshairs of their microscope lenses, with attention on BMAA. One team, from Oregon Health & Science University, fed high doses of BMAA to monkeys with the result that they began to exhibit symptoms similar to those found in the Chamorro afflicted with lytico-bodig.

The studies were quickly challenged on the basis that it would take exceptional amounts of cycad flour to provoke neurodegenerative symptoms, and unlikely that any humans—or monkeys—on Guam would ever indulge to that extent. Interest in the subject soon died off until it was revived at the turn of the century by an ethnobotanist named Paul Cox who was at the time Director of the National Tropical Botanical Garden on Hawaii.

Cox, a large man with a quick and eclectic mind, was studying bats. He knew about the cluster on Guam and knew that the Chamorro loved to eat bats. He also knew that symptoms existed almost exclusively in older members of the tribe. It turned out that one of the culinary delights of the Chamorro, flying foxes the natives called *fanihi*, was cooked in coconut milk and eaten whole (bones and all). The bats were much sought after and quickly hunted to extinction on the island—explaining why younger people exhibited no symptoms of lytico-bodig. The bats foraged on cycad seeds, so each delicacy was loaded with BMAA through a process called biomagnification. The final, and critical, piece of thinking was that the cycad trees got their nourishment through their coralloid roots which harbored cyanobacteria and provided nitrogen to the plants, as well as the neurotoxin BMAA.

Teaming up with Sandra Banack from California State University at Fullerton, a bat expert, and Susan Murch, an amino acid expert from the University of Guelph, Cox then analyzed small samples from three flying fox specimens from Guam and found that all carried massive amounts of BMAA. They subsequently found similar high concentrations in a further study of 21 additional flying fox specimens.[105] Cox was respected in his field of ethnobotany but was an outsider to neurology, so when he published the results of their study in 2003 the scientific world gave out a great yawn.

But Cox, determined to follow his hunch, gained access to brain tissue samples from six Chamorro (collected by previous neurologists) who had died of lytico-bodig, in a double blind study using thirteen Canadians in a control group who had passed away with no signs of neurodegeneration, found that the Chamorro and two Canadians had significant quantities of BMAA in the brain tissue, whereas the control group had none. On breaking the blind, they discovered that two of the Canadians with BMAA in their brains had died of Alzheimer's disease.

With compelling evidence in hand, Cox faced a conundrum: how could the Canadians have been exposed to BMAA when they lived so far from, and had never visited, Guam? Here he made an intuitive the leap; it had to be microbes that were punching out the toxin. And those microbes had to be among the most common forms of all: cyanobacteria.

Cox began to assemble a consortium of over fifty top scientists and researchers throughout the world to help him focus on the human health effects of BMAA, thinking that exposure to this toxin might be a risk factor for ALS, Alzheimer's, and other neurodegenerative diseases. His quest led him to found the Institute for Ethnomedicine in

Jackson Hole, Wyoming, (now called the Brain Chemistry Labs), with a laser focus on human brain diseases.

More clusters

The work by Cox intrigued Dr. Elijah Stommel, a neurologist at the Dartmouth-Hitchcock Medical Center in Lebanon, New Hampshire. Stommel was beginning to see a large number of patients with ALS and decided to statistically canvass the area around Dartmouth to see if there were any clusters of the disease. He found that people living on and around Mascoma Lake in nearby Enfield had a twenty-five times better chance of contracting the disease than the general population. And every summer, the pristine lake exhibited blooms—exploding populations—of cyanobacteria.

Mascoma Lake was not alone. As Stommel expanded his reach he discovered other clusters around Lake Champlain and near Bangor, Maine. A later study of fifty lakes in New Hampshire showed that nearly all lakes had cyanobacteria blooms. In other words, cyanobacteria were ubiquitous throughout the state. And in a way, Paul Cox's insistence that the problem originated in microbes was answered.

However, being a scientist, Stommel admitted that there was much to be known about the trigger mechanism for neurodegenerative diseases including genetic predisposition and other elements of risk taken in various levels of exposure. In addition, there was another looming question: if breathed in or ingested as part of diet, how could the toxin cross the blood-brain barrier? In other words, it could get in the blood but how could it get into the brain?

Blood-brain barrier

Brain cells are fed by proteins, which are formed by a complex process (like a recipe) in which transfer RNA, a very specific enzyme, picks up an amino acid and matches it to a codon (one of three nucleotides) that starts or stops protein synthesis. There are twenty known amino acids. Once organized into proper sequence, called folding, the chain of amino acids then is a completely formed protein and is incorporated into the brain cell.

BMAA has the moniker of nonproteingenic because it does not belong to the standard family of twenty amino acids. But, in the process of building a protein chain, BMAA sometimes is mistaken for serine (one of the twenty) and is incorporated into the protein chain. (Levodopa—L-DOPA— is another nonproteingenic amino acid that sometimes attaches to tyrosine.) But since BMAA is an interloper, it can cause the protein to misfold and clump into a larger aggregate which is one marker for the presence of neurodegenerative disease.

Susan Ackerman, a neuroscientist at the Howard Hughes Institute, studying the effects of neuronal changes on the aging brain, published a paper in 2006 about how misincorporated proteins led to neurodegeneration in mice. And to finalize the process, in 2011 a paper was presented by two Australian members of Cox's consortium, Ken Rodgers and Rachael Dunlop, at the International ALS/Motor Neuron Disease Symposium explained how the serine amino acid could pick up BMAA and incorporate it into a protein, followed by protein misfolding and cell death.[106, 107]

A second and potentially deadly outcome of exposure to cyanobacterial blooms is serious liver disease. A toxin produced by cyanobacteria of the genus *Mycrocystis* can trigger primary liver cancer.[108] Decades of research have confirmed the link between the cyanotoxin *Microcystin* and liver disease.

Doubt abounds

As noted earlier, the work of Cox and his consortium was received with skepticism among many members of the scientific community who had been studying neurodegenerative disease for years.

For example, an ophthalmological researcher who studies neuroscience in Canada, had an alternative cycad toxin in mind called sterol glucosides which he found causes neurodegenerative changes in mice. He did not find such changes cause by BMAA in six mice, concluding that BMAA must not be able to cross the blood-brain barrier. And other researchers, using different methods to identify elements associated with brain diseases, were unable to come to Cox's conclusion.[109]

In 2016, Cox and his team together with scientists at the Department of Neurology at the University of Miami found that chronic dietary exposure to BMAA triggers the formation of amyloid plaque and neurofibrillary tangles, the two hallmarks of Alzheimer's disease, in vervets on the island of St. Kitts whereas control animals not exposed to BMAA did not develop such neuropathology.[110] These animals share the APOe4 gene, which in humans significantly increases the risk of Alzheimer's.

A critical literature review published by toxicologists at the University of Mississippi concluded that BMAA causes neurodegeneration in laboratory animals,[111] but their conclusion was contradicted by a more recent literature review published by researchers at EPA, in 2017, whose conclusion is unambiguous: "The review concludes that the hypothesis of a causal BMAA neurodegenerative disease relationship is not supported by existing data."[112]

Pharmaceutical companies have spent billions of dollars based on an observation that in patients with ALS there is always the presence of beta-amyloids which, when aggregated become amyloids. But the data from Lake Mascoma and studies from Guam lead one to conclude that there may be a connection between BMAA, as a by-product of cyanobacterial uptake in very high concentrations, and that the subject is worthy of continuing study.

Given the variety of good research, the most likely conclusion is that Parkinson's, ALS and Alzheimer's are triggered by any one or a combination of many factors, including genetic predisposition, diet and lack of exercise, as well as environmental toxins consumed through the food chain. As is true with many cases of disease, aging and the efficacy of the human immune system play a large role in determining the pathway from good health to various maladies, but in the case of BMAA identification, leading to elimination or mitigation of one of the triggers, is worth continuing the effort on multiple fronts.

Dolphin necropsy

Research mice were a far cry from humans, and research continued in a laboratory setting on the BMAA connection with diseases of the brain until 2018 when a group of scientists, mainly from Florida, dissected the brains of dolphins after beaching themselves, possibly due to loss of navigational ability. 2017 had brought about the highest levels of toxic mycrocystins since 2012 and the hypothesis was that a portion of the dolphins' brains may have been affected by some form of deterioration or dementia.[113] Dolphins use echolocation to move through the water. Emitting a series of audible clicks, and timing the return of sound bounced off solid or moving objects gives the dolphin a mental image of its location and, to some degree, the nature of the object from the bounce back. There is also the possibility that the earth's magnetic field functions as a sort of GPS for dolphins, but the science in that regard is unsettled at best.[114]

Dolphins are a sentinel species for marine study. They are apex predators, eating and living at the top of the food chain. Their diet consists of smaller fish that tend to eat clams, oysters and smaller occupants of the benthic habitat.

The dolphins studied came from the Indian River Lagoon where high levels of cyanobacteria had been released down the St. Lucie River—with the dolphins ingesting and bioaccumulating high amounts of BMAA. In addition to being mammals, the dolphin's brain is highly compartmentalized, much like the human brain, and scientists know which areas control various musculoskeletal functions. By measuring the amount of BMAA in certain brain regions of the stranded dolphins, scientists believed they could isolate the navigational region, the auditory complex, to see if that part of the dead dolphin's brain was compromised.

Seven of the dolphins were found in areas of Florida known to have recurrent harmful algae blooms, and seven were found in Cape Cod Bay in Massachusetts. The Florida specimens, all bottlenose dolphins, were found either floating or beached. Using carefully documented techniques, the scientists found that the Florida dolphins' brains had three times the concentrations of BMAA when compared to the Massachusetts dolphins. External observation showed no anomalies from normal, but in brain tissue in the auditory complex, when carefully sliced and stained, those areas relating to navigation also showed cellular aging, levels of β - amyloid as well as a high level of methylmercury (MeHg), (a highly toxic substance found in large quantities in Florida's Everglades) in dolphins studied. With combined methylmercury and BMAA, the scientists concluded that there was a high risk of dementia.[115]

The dolphin study is not directly connected to human

disease, but raises concerns about the risk of chronic exposure to BMAA associated with cyanobacterial blooms in coastal estuaries, particularly as it relates to the mammalian brain.

Climate change and harmful algae blooms

As the scientific evidence that the planet was warming spread beyond the climate science community, studies began on the impact on saltwater marine ecosystems. The links were hard to prove because, once again, correlation does not equal causality. But marine biologists know with certainty that warmer oceans have coincidentally increased acidification leading to the bleaching of coral reefs throughout the world down to Monroe County in southwest Florida, the only coral reef in the continental United States.

The connection here goes back to the Mesozoic era when two eukaryotic phytoplankton were competing for dominance, dinoflagellates against cocolithophorids. As the pH of water dropped during that period, the cocolithophorids were less able to extract calcium from the water. The population dropped and the dinoflagellates moved into the econiche.[116] This scenario is being repeated today as the calcium carbonate ($CaCO_3$) in the planet's oceans is dropping due to higher acidity from a lower pH.

Studies of fresh water ecosystems has been going on for decades, but in many cases there is a paucity of base line water quality standards set for many inland waters, particularly lakes. Rivers have gained attention because they end up in estuaries in the Gulf. Base line standards are necessary to determine the rate of either deterioration or improvement in water quality as measured over time.

Global warming will probably increase the nutrient base for harmful algae. A heating planet will cause warmer waters, changes to the vertical mixing in the water column and evaporation at the surface contributing to eutrophication and the demise of a variety of microorganisms that provide nutrients for naturally occurring algae like *K. brevis* and cyanobacteria. This subject was studied extensively in a 2012 paper by J. M. O'Neil and collaborators, the abstract of which stated: "While the interactive effects of future eutrophication and climate change on harmful cyanobacterial blooms are complex, much of the current knowledge suggests that these processes are likely to enhance the magnitude and frequency of the [outbreaks]."[117] The authors concluded that with higher temperatures cyanobacteria would thrive. One poster child for this process is Lake Okeechobee.

A word of caution is necessary here. It is extremely difficult to isolate the effects of climate change from other factors such as leaking septic tanks, stormwater, urban runoff, and fertilizers. As baseline data increases, it may be possible to extract single elements, but at the present level of knowledge any conclusions drawn about a connection between global warming and an increase in harmful algae blooms should be regarded as conjecture.

The differentiation between salt water (red tide) dinoflagelates and cyanobacteria in both salt and fresh water ecosystems is a critical distinction because global warming will have entirely different effects upon the ecosystem of each.

In the case of salt water, it will lead to rising sea levels and an elevation in coastal water tables, leading to the further likelihood of compromised ageing septic tanks and increased stormwater runoff allowing *K. brevis* to thrive on increased nutrients pouring into the Gulf.

And, as the planet warms, there will be a preponderance of female sea turtles like Dorothy, born in the beaches around the world as the average temperature of the sand rises above 82° Fahrenheit.

The science is very strong on one point regarding fresh water cyanobacteria. In the case of impoundments, such as ponds and lakes, global warming will lead to increased growth of cyanobacteria, many varieties of which thrive and happily reproduce in warmer water temperatures. This borne out by growth and eutrophication as we have seen in Lake Okeechobee, increased levels of scum in canals and inland lakes and ponds, and a lengthening of window in which blooms thrive causing a reduction in human recreational opportunities.

Cyanobacteria redux

A great deal is known about human health consequences and outbreaks of red tide. The subject has been carefully studied for years. Monitoring and identification systems are in place throughout Florida, the best of all states bordering the Gulf of Mexico. Notification and warnings to coastal communities are coordinated among state, county and local authorities, and are both timely and effective.

That is not necessarily true with toxic cyanobacteria in high concentrations. It is a relative newcomer to southwest Florida's estuaries. The consequences are still being studied, and there is enough uncertainty and controversy surrounding the science to keep government authorities cautious on overcommitting resources to the problem. However, if the consequences from exposure to BMAA are as potentially dire as the research indicates, with life-ending manifestations of neurodegeneration, government will need to step in quickly and authoritatively.

The significance of BMAA in southwest Florida is simple. While beta amyloids and tangles are present in vervet monkeys exposed to BMAA, and in Chamorro villagers who eat a BMAA-rich diet, many other causes are likely to trigger neurodegeneration in the human brain, so the totality of the causes are still unclear to medical science. BMAA exposure may only be a small path, of tremendous consequence to villagers in Guam, but not of overwhelming significance elsewhere. But, most importantly, assuming that BMAA is also a contributor to deterioration of brain cells, the cause is clear enough to merit immediate action to prevent outbreaks of cyanobacterial blooms. This is right in the backyard of everyone living in southwest Florida and it can be mitigated in the short-term and eliminated over a period of decades.

While Florida's identification and notification systems

in place work smoothly, the state has avoided looking into the reasons why algae outbreaks occur in the first place. In the case of red tide, the initiation phase is the least well understood and there may be way of interrupting the sequence that leads to an outbreak. In the case of cyanobacteria, the causes are pretty well established from worldwide research efforts, but for some reason the state has been unwilling to open a full and complete discussion on how to choke off the well-known elements leading to cyanobacteria blooms. This is the subject of the next chapter.

CHAPTER 8

Sonorous Silence and the Politics of Florida

◆———·•◆•·———◆

Florida has always been reluctant to face controversial issues head-on. Some wags believe it is partially a reflection of the idea that Florida is really five different states, culturally and demographically. The northern tier, along the panhandle to Jacksonville, is populated by a large number of retirees, from military backgrounds, and people who depend upon the military bases stretched out along the northern tier of the state. Moving south to the central part of the state, Orlando is a sprawling metropolis and rapidly growing melting-pot of ethnicities and interests. The southeast coast is populated by emigres from New York and expatriates from Cuba, South America and the Caribbean. And southwest Florida is comprised of a combination of retirees and younger people, with a decidedly conservative bent.

The fifth Florida is found all over the state, outside the metropolitan areas like Miami and Orlando, consisting of native families, farmers and ranchers, and rural folks who are happy to eschew the other four Floridas. The state legislature, the most powerful political force in the state, is controlled by the fifth Florida. By nature and tradition, it is always cautious, chary of regulation and resentful of federal mandates.

The state legislature is also protective of its prerogatives and always looking for ways to expand its influence. Power in the legislature lies in the leadership, in the Speaker of the House and the President of the Senate. The Speaker has the power to appoint committee chairs who advance the bills which the speaker supports and has to power to keep bills from coming out of committee to the floor. The leadership is selected four years ahead of time, and assuming the nominees are re-elected, come to power but are beholden to those who selected them from among the forty senators and one hundred twenty house members. About 3,000 bills per year are proposed but only 300 make it to the governor's desk.

Another fountainhead of power lies in lobbyists. The most powerful group is health care. With a growing number of retirees, the industry wants little interference with ongoing provider operations and drug pricing. The second group is home building and real estate development. Their desire is to preserve the *status quo* insofar as possible, to be able to plan ahead for long-term investments. And third is agriculture seeking to preserve their low profit margin businesses, with as little additional costs as necessary.

A brief recounting of major milestones, in Florida's ongoing battle to preserve local options over federal dictates and intervention, offers a series of good examples as to how the process works. But first a little background.

FAWPCA

Elected governor, in 1966, and advised by Nathaniel Reed, an environmental advocate and scion of the family that developed Hobe Sound, Claude Kirk was determined to prepare Florida, for the onslaught of visitors and new residents. He convinced the legislature to pass the Florida Air and Water Pollution Control Act (FAWPCA), in 1967. It was a landmark bill "to conserve, protect and improve the quality of Florida's waters for a variety of purposes, including public water supplies and preservation of wildlife."[118]

The bill gave the Florida Department of Environmental Protection (FDEP) broad powers to regulate and enforce water quality standards throughout the state, and judicial remedies, including fines and even jail time for violators. It has been amended a number of times, once to require coordination with the federal Clean Water Act and again to conform to the terms of the Federal National Pollution Discharge Elimination System (NPDES) to allow industrial and agricultural permits to discharge pollution into the surface waters of the state. It was a boon for polluters, because Florida now has over 23,000 NPDES permits, over 10% of the nation's total.[119]

Still on the books today as Florida Statutes (F.S.), Sections 403.011 to 403.0611, the powerful provisions set forth in the FAWPCA have faded with time and FDEP no longer takes advantage of the mandate given it by Governor Kirk, Nathaniel Reed and the state legislature, because as the decades passed it became clear that conforming to high standards of pollution management and control would be an expensive proposition given the rapidly growing population and the proliferation of entrenched and powerful special interests.

Chiles' Task Force

Governor Lawton Chiles created the Governor's Commission for a Sustainable South Florida (GCSSF), in 1994. As the Comprehensive Everglades Restoration Plan (CERP), a program popular with the voters, was going through a lengthy planning process and was only a nascent thought in the Congress at the time (it finally passed in 2000), the state legislature decided to create the Everglades Forever Act of 1994, to codify the state's commitment to restore and protect the Everglades ecosystem. Following that, with an executive order, Chiles created a blue-ribbon commission populated by affected interests including agriculture, environmental, Native American tribes, developers, urban interests, and regulatory agencies. The idea was to put everyone in one room to resolve CERP-related conflicts insofar as possible.

The group had an illustrious membership representing all aspects of the Florida economy, with particular attention given to farmers whose main concern was preservation of their water allocations so they could obtain interim financing from lenders, looking carefully at the availability of water, and commercial fishermen who were losing as much as eighteen million dollars a year due to shellfish poisoning. Richard Pettigrew, former Speaker of the Florida House of Representatives, was named chair. Over the five years of its existence, the commission produced a number of reports exhaustively and collectively describing the problems confronting the economy and environment.

The first report to the governor, in October 1995, set out one hundred ten recommendations, directly confronting some of the thorny issues along the fault lines of divided political opinion. "... the Commission agreed that past water management activities in south Florida, geared predominantly toward satisfying urban and agricultural demands have often ignored many needs of the natural system, particularly in drought conditions."[120] It went on: "The Commission, under the consensus approach, has strongly recommended that the South Florida Water Management District establish minimum flows and levels describing when withdrawals from a water source must cease."[121]

A good idea but the problem, of course, was that the U.S. Army Corps of Engineers (USACE) was responsible for the safety of the residents in towns south of the lake and had no choice but to maintain the lake at what it regarded as safe levels, regardless of the SFWMD might want or recommend.

The 1995 report also stated, in the bluntest terms, that the south Florida ecosystem, and particularly the Everglades, was unsustainable and on a trajectory toward disaster. As a result of public pressure, Chiles asked the commission to continue for the next three years, to provide guidance and oversight of the over one hundred recommendations set forth in the commission's first report. The emphasis on Everglade's restoration was always on the front burner with organizations like the Everglades Foundation, run by powerful advocates with a substantial budget keeping the vision in front of the public and elected officials.

A second report, in August 1996, by the Commission had, as its central showpiece, a series of recommendations setting forth the criteria for a restudy of C&SF project, noting that the manner in which water resources were being managed was simply not serving the interests of all parties fairly and proportionally. And, once again, the issue of water quality was brought into the discussion.

Wetherell task force

As noted earlier, money flowed from both the federal and state budgets in response to moments of crisis and dried up as the crisis passed. With clear evidence that outbreaks of red tide were increasing in intensity, duration, and coverage, another notable attempt was made to deal with the problem when, in 1997, the Florida Harmful Algae Bloom Task Force (FHABTF) was formed by Virginia Wetherell, at the time Secretary of FDEP under Governor Chiles.

Chiles' main interest was in keeping Florida's economy healthy, with less regard to environmental issues and Wetherell reflected his views. She regarded the role of FDEP as that of facilitator, to help developers understand and obey the rules. The department had been created after a merger of the Department of Natural Resources and Department of Environmental Regulation, and Wetherell set the early tone, to the consternation of many staff members of the merged departments. She was heavily criticized by environmental groups but did support Preservation 2000—the long-standing land acquisition program and initiated the FHABTF, so her tenure had to be regarded as neutral at best.

The group did not first convene until 1999, under newly elected Governor Jeb Bush. It was composed of a broad cross-section of environmental advocates, developers and political wannabees, and met for two years to receive and publicize a series of staff reports on the increasing problem of algal blooms. Then, in 2001, the state legislature abruptly defunded the program and it slipped quietly into the background, with limited funding from various state agencies.

The apparent success and acceptance of the GCSSF

should have brought into question the need for a second commission, with many of the same goals. The two groups had overlapping responsibilities, and both were competing for appropriations, in the state legislature. In addition, during the months of March through August, from 1997 through 2001, Florida's coastal estuaries were entirely free of red tide. The legislature defunded the FHABTF in 2001 because algae blooms began to take a back seat to other priorities affecting the ecosystem, but a task force of members continued to meet, with money from the Florida Marine Research Institute.

Despite its short life span, a careful analysis of the statutory responsibilities of the FHABTF is instructive, as we consider how the state was beginning to gingerly approach the issue of algal blooms:

Review the status and adequacy of information for monitoring physical, chemical, biological, economic and public health factors affecting harmful algae blooms in Florida;

Develop research and monitoring priorities for harmful algal blooms in Florida;

Develop recommendations that can be implemented by state and local governments to develop a response plan to predict, mitigate and control the effects of harmful algal blooms;

Make recommendations to the Florida Marine Research Institute by October 1, 1999, for research, detection monitoring, prediction, mitigation and control of harmful algal blooms in Florida.

The mission of the FHABTF never really addressed locating and dealing with sources of nutrient pollution. An underlying assumption seems to be that the blooms would occur naturally and that no amount of time and money thrown at the sources would result in an actionable and meaningful conclusion.

Deftly deflecting the Clean Water Act

Another example of the reluctance to tackle tough environmental issues, almost in defiance of Governor Kirk's FAWPCA, occurred, in 1998, when the federal Environmental Protection Agency (EPA), after being sued by environmental groups, declared that Florida was violating the Clean Water Act (CWA), by not setting hard, numeric nutrient standards, limiting pollution of its waterbodies. Florida had until 2004 to comply. The standard in place at the time was a typical poster child for procrastination: "In no case shall nutrient concentrations of a body of water be altered so as to cause an imbalance in natural populations of aquatic flora and fauna." [122] The word "imbalance" was never defined.

In addition, setting numeric thresholds would be the equivalent of establishing a water quality standard (WQS) which, if violated over a period of time, would lead to a requirement, under the CWA, to establish a Total Maximum

Daily Load (TMDL), for the affected water body. But, setting standards and putting them into effect were two different things, because there was no requirement under the current federal law that a state must implement a TMDL, even after being established. This loophole was ratified and codified a year later, in the Florida Watershed Restoration Act of 1999 (FWRA).

The order from EPA, with a 2004 deadline, was acceptable as a settlement by Governor Jeb Bush with his brother sitting in the White House, because five years was a long time to find ways of softening the terms of settlement into something more acceptable given the vocal objections to numeric criteria by business, local sewer districts, farmers and individuals who associated such standards with higher costs. But even more relevant was the background fact that no federal or state law required full implementation of an existing TMDL.

Disgusted by inaction, a group of environmental organizations again sued the EPA, in 2008, for failing to enforce adoption of numeric standards by the State of Florida. FDEP, stung by the 2008 lawsuit, could slip the noose by simply changing the way waterbodies in Florida were classified, and any WQS promulgated would have to be reviewed and redefined under the new classification system. The idea was supported by the Florida Farm Bureau, Associated Industries, Florida League of Cities and a group set up to support the classification changes called Don't Tax Florida. Members of all four groups were upset when considering the expenses associated with cleaning up Florida's polluted waterbodies.

Under the existing definition, Class III waterbodies were those which could maintain healthy populations of fish and wildlife and be well adapted for human recreation. FDEP's new classification system would add to the existing Class III two new classifications: HU4 and HU5. The first would be for waterbodies suited for fishing and human recreation to the point of splashing (but not swimming). The second new classification would prohibit fishing and limit human contact due to the presence of toxins in the canal or lake under question. A third new classification, HU3, would apply to all waterbodies not included in HU4 and HU5.

The politics of deflection were nakedly at work to avoid setting numeric standards, but the idea failed because of the public outcry against the new classifications

After the hue and cry died down, FDEP went ahead and suggested creation of a new Class III Limited designation which would apply to parts of the built environment like roadside canals and storm water diversion ditches, and would allow the consumption of fish caught in those canals but no full-body human immersion, which was eventually adopted.[123]

Another wrinkle to the new system was the idea that there could be different classifications within the same watershed. In other words, inland segments of a river or stream could have a less stringent classification than downstream segments. This would require that somehow dirty water needed to be cleaned up as it flowed before it could be discharged into sections with a higher classification. The idea of uniform numeric standards throughout a waterbody raised a howl of protests among municipalities, counties and sewer districts, but was heavily supported by coastal residents who felt that their estuaries and beaches would suffer.

EPA finally entered into a settlement agreement that permitted the state to set its own numeric standards, but the state let the deadline pass with no action. EPA then issued standards, but for some reason exempted a large part of southwest Florida. Burdened by the federal dictate, the state finally issued its own standards which represented a threshold but not a cap on nutrient pollution. And, the state allowed the threshold value to exceed the published limits once every three years, whereas federal regulations required annual measurements and continuous compliance.

Then, in a curious memo dripping with duplicity, FDEP issued a report that same year stating:

"Freshwater algal blooms (HABs) are increasing in frequency, duration, and magnitude and therefore may be a significant threat to surface drinking water resources and recreational areas. Abundant populations of blue-green algae, some of them potentially toxigenic, have been found statewide in numerous lakes and rivers. In additions, measured concentrations of cyanotoxins – a few of them of above the suggested guideline levels – have been reported in finished water from some drinking water facilities." [124]

By 2018, of the 4,393 waterbodies reviewed and assessed in the State of Florida, 2,440 had been declared "impaired." [125] Claude Kirk would be ashamed.

This story chronicling the extent to which the state went to avoid numeric standards is an example of ways of working around federally mandated standards. There would be costs involved, running in the billions of dollars. And Florida has always been a proud, low-tax state. The options were to take partial steps or to completely avoid the issues and do nothing at all, and avoidance of the cost of cleaning up impaired waters was always at the forefront of arguments to do less or to do nothing at all.

Partial steps

Another case illustrating the haphazard nature of Florida's approach to nutrient pollution of its streams and rivers, the Caloosahatchee, below the Franklin Lock, has a TMDL for total nitrogen (TN) both organic and inorganic, which is incorporated into a Basin Management Action Plan (BMAP). About 61% of nutrient loading from sources in the watershed originate in Lake Okeechobee with other identified non-point sources at 24%. The balance comes from natural runoff. But even a reduction from non-point sources, including fertilizer runoff and failing septic tanks and agriculture draining into the lake, would not make a significant difference, because there was never a TMDL posted for the Caloosahatchee in its entirety.

Do nothing at all

To deal with prevention also invites an analysis of causes, an area fraught with a clear lack of leadership, routinely sidestepped by the politics of deflection to other subjects, as a way to do nothing at all. A perfect example of this strategy is how the legislature dealt with Amendment 5 to the state constitution.

The amendment was passed in 1995 by nearly 70% of the voters, and provided that "(t)hose in the Everglades Agricultural Area who cause water pollution within the Everglades Protection Area or the Everglades Agricultural Area shall be primarily responsible for the costs of the abatement of that pollution."

It was up to the legislature to enact enabling bills, but nothing was done, until 2003, when the state Supreme Court entered the picture again by ruling against the 1996 opinion of Attorney General Robert Butterworth that ". . .while the legislature may enact provisions implementing Amendment #5, the amendment itself establishes an obligation on polluters of the Everglades to pay the costs of abating such pollution *irrespective of legislative action* [italics mine]." [126] Enacting legislation was never passed, and the 2003 court opinion drove a stake into the heart of Amendment 5.

In the most obvious way of thinking about this case,

political maneuvering was replaced by outright obstinate opposition. Another interpretation of the events between 1996 and 2003 might be that the legislature, in its efforts to duck direct responsibility for defying the intent of the voters as expressed in Amendment 5, used the courts in the hope that a judicial ruling might bury the issue and prevent the curtain from being pulled back to expose the real wizard.

Questioning the FWRI data base

One of the most effective ways to delay action on controversial issues is to question the science identifying and studying the problem as was the case with early reports from scientists dispatched to do on-site data collection and analysis of red tide along Florida's coast. Almost all of their work was integrated into the Fish and Wildlife Research Institute (FWRI) data base, outlining the dates, by month, of red tide outbreaks. However, FWRI warned that its data base was fraught with problems, due to inconsistencies in sampling and reporting methods.

This line of argument is of genuine concern, particularly to those scientists involved in analyzing the steady increase in the frequency and duration of outbreaks, since 1995, and those advising the 2008 Management and Response Plan. This cautious approach could be read in different ways: First, it could be a reasonable and legitimate concern that sampling techniques were not standardized or adjusted and that a degree of bias exists in all the data sets, based upon the fact that much of the information was collected after initiation of a bloom but with some uncertainty as to the exact phase of the bloom. This is reactive sampling and does not necessarily take into account factors like the depth of the water column.

Second, it could be argued that by throwing cold water on its own published data, the FWRI was being overly cautious. In other words, don't rely on our records when drawing conclusions about red tide outbreaks. That is a reasonable argument to make about some of the earlier data but as the outbreaks became annual events, more standardized sampling techniques came into play.

The same gap exists between those who believe that urban runoff and failing septic tanks are the main source of nutrients for red tide in its growth phase, and those who doubt that terrestrial sources have anything to do with nourishing red tide, because measurement on non-point source runoff is hard to measure reliably and consistently. The reality probably lies somewhere in the fact that *K. brevis*, with its grazing ability, is able to access multiple sources of nutrients, some of which may already be in the water column and some of which may come pouring off the land. Further complicating that argument is a question as to how much runoff is natural and how much is anthropogenic. However, drawing back the curtain on the wizard, there is a growing consensus that in both cases—the reliability of FWRI data or the impact of urban runoff on red tide bloom growth— there is sufficient evidence to regard both as moving toward settled science.

And the beat goes on

Further recitation, of the obstacles toward identifying and dealing with the relationship of land-based nutrient runoff and the exacerbation of *K. brevis* and cyanobacteria blooms, is repetitive and unneeded. The problem is a lack of political will to make the necessary changes, by enacting regulation to deal with land-based runoff that fuels both dinoflagellates like *K. brevis* and cyanobacteria.

Most recently, measures to deal with water quality issues, during the 2019 legislative session, met with failure. There were thirteen bills proposing the strengthening of environmental controls. Four were particularly relevant, introduced to (1) reduce fertilizer runoff,[127] (2) inspect and regulate septic tanks,[128] (3) make storm water management recommendations,[129] and (4) control the use of biosolids.[130]

Each of the four bills above dealt with a separate problem. In the first instance, there has been an ongoing battle between the state and numerous municipalities about how to control fertilizers. The state has mandated that cities and counties cannot ban the sale of lawn fertilizers but has produced a model ordinance that minimizes use during Florida's wet season, allows local control of how near to ponds and lakes fertilizer can be applied, requires soil deficiency analysis, before applying phosphorous, and sets a minimum on slow-release nitrogen. So far, over one hundred municipalities have adopted local ordinances to control application of nitrogen and phosphorous. The rules apply to residential lots, but golf courses, public property like athletic fields, and agricultural operations are all exempted.

In the second instance, control of septic tanks, there is no inventory as to location and age of tanks throughout the state. Following the 2012 repeal of a state mandate for periodic inspections, and despite bills introduced nearly every year in Tallahassee, there remains no appetite to have regular inspections of septic tanks. In addition, most septic tanks have no way of filtering out nitrogen which flows directly into the watershed through the tank's drainage field—in Florida about seventeen pounds per person each year.

There are 2.7 million tanks statewide, but the number affecting coastal watersheds is not known. The cost to replace every septic tank in the state has been estimated at $1 billion per year for twenty years. To replace tanks that do not meet current standards is estimated to run between $12,000–$20,000 for replacements with nitrogen removing capability. $5,000 to hook into a new sewer system for each home, but that does not include the cost to municipalities and sewer districts to run new pipes and add sufficient capacity which is $15,000–$20,000 per home.

In addition, replacement and monitoring of septic tanks is a divisive issue. The cost, particularly in rural areas, is the most obvious bone of contention, but there is also a pushback, mainly from the industry, about the role septic tanks play in waste runoff.

Much of the problem could be addressed by mandating periodic inspections and pump-outs. A bill passed, in 2010, requiring regular inspections, but was repealed in 2012, during the anti-regulatory frenzy of Governor Rick Scott, as complaints poured in about the cost of pumping out tanks on a regular basis. Similar bills introduced in the state legislature since then have never made it out of committee to the floor, of either the House or the Senate for a vote of the entire legislature.

In the third case, storm water, in most of south Florida's municipalities, is handled by antiquated systems. For example, the storm water drain system for the City of Naples was built in the 1950s, shunting untreated water through direct outfalls into the city's bays and the Gulf of Mexico. Drainage from impervious surfaces like roofs of larger houses, roads and parking lots is rich in nutrients and organic matter such as grass clippings. There are no up-to-date statewide standards for storm water management, and compliance is based upon best management practices (BMPs), not by regular, measured sampling.

Finally, biosolids, known as Class B municipal sewage sludge, come in dried, bulk form. Florida generates nearly 350,000 tons of the stuff which either goes to landfills or is used as fertilizer sometimes indiscriminately. The annual phosphorous and nitrogen loads come close to one thousand tons and two thousand tons respectively. There are currently no regulations as to how and where biosolids can be applied. The 2019 bill was originally designed to prevent biosolids from being spread on pasture lands but was later absorbed into another bill that controlled when, rather than where, biosolids could be applied, and delayed from 2020 to 2022 an important provision to keep biosolids out of the water table.

Ron DeSantis, a former Republican congressman and graduate of Yale University and Harvard Law School, ran for governor, in 2018, on a platform of addressing the water quality problems of Florida. And, unlike many politicians, once elected, he followed through on campaign promises in the early days of his administration, by appointing two task forces to recommend solutions to the burgeoning problem.

In April 2019, he appointed a five-member task force of academic heavyweights, to study blue-green algae and to work with Noah Valenstein, Secretary of FDEP. Taken together, both Valenstein and the task force members had respectable environmental chops.

At the group's second meeting, Tom Fisk of FDEP put a fine point on the matter. "In general our approach is to put the watershed on a diet as to what is coming into [Lake Okeechobee] and, as long as you're seeing progress there, then start bringing in and looking at what is coming in from the sediment and shift your focus."[131] His point was well-taken, because the legacy phosphorous in the lake would have to be dealt with, but only after reducing the levels of input from the Kissimmee Lakes and Everglades Agriculture Area. The task force also was in agreement that agriculture and ranching were the primary sources of nutrient loading into the watershed.

The task force has been mindful of the cost of solutions, and realistic in its approach. The main focus has been on identifying levels of concentration that lead to human health problems, and on the long-term effects of chronic exposure to the toxin. A secondary focus has been on ways to monitor and measure the level of toxins present without the usual warning signs, of visible pollution and odor.

Environmentalists have tried to bring more of the group's attention to a lack of enforcement of the voluntary BMPs agreed to by agricultural interests, and to encourage better record-keeping, as to the results of compliance according to the practices in place and used by farmers.

After appointing the blue-green algae task force, Governor DeSantis then reactivated the state's red tide task force. The group had originally been formed under Governor Chiles and then continued under Governor Bush, until it was defunded by the legislature in 2001. It then limped along with funding from the Fish and Wildlife Research Institute, until its final collapse, in 2004.

In its rebirth fifteen years later, the group of eleven scientists and prominent citizens, all with experience in natural resource management and public health, would be funded by the Florida Fish and Wildlife Conservation Commission's Center for Red Tide Research, at $4.8 million for the first year.

The hope with both task forces is that science will prevail and political considerations, while necessarily part of the deliberative process, will be put aside during the creation of recommendations for legislative consideration. And equally important is that existing regulations, in effect, be enforced by state agencies empowered to do so, going back to 1967 and the days of Claude Kirk.

CONCLUSION

To write about the history of red tide and blue-green algae invites the opportunity to comment on solutions. That is risky business given the fact that the science is constantly developing and that the political landscape in Florida changes every two or four years. However, there are some parts to the story that are clear enough to remark on.

The early history of red tide outbreaks, in the Gulf of Mexico, is checkered with anecdotal and personal observations. There were no credible data sets to give Ingersoll and Taylor a scientific basis for workable hypotheses; it was pretty much a matter of intuition. During the early years, the red tide phenomenon remained a concern of a select few scientists, all employed by agencies of the federal government. There was no independently funded work being done, until 1945, when, after three decades of relative calm, the southwest coastal estuaries of Florida were blanketed by a huge. aquatic bloom from Captiva to Cape Romano.

Solutions—begin with prevention of K. brevis

The first problem to tackle is the lack of focus on preventing red tide algae outbreaks. The phenomenon is increasing worldwide, in areas that mirror the geophysical profile of southwest Florida, and throughout the world where scientists, regulatory authorities and political leaders are trying to deal with the problem in innovative and effective ways. These efforts need to be carefully examined for application in the Gulf of Mexico, the area where *K. brevis* survives at threshold levels and then periodically explodes. While Florida has the strongest detection and notification system of all the Gulf coast states, the solution cannot be limited to southwest Florida, because blooms periodically occur in almost every estuary, along the coast from Mexico to the Florida Keys—a total of 5,095 miles of shoreline.

There are some promising technologies to control outbreaks. They are mainly coming from laboratories, but once out in the open waters of the Gulf, they become extremely difficult to administer safely into limited areas. Experiments have been conducted in canals and enclosed areas but, based upon the 1957 copper sulfate outcome by the Bureau of Fisheries, there is little likelihood of reliable and scalable chemical substances or mechanisms becoming widely available.

Prevention is possible. The initialization phase of *K. brevis* blooms is the least understood but when it enters the second, or growth phase, as the bloom expands into a larger more concentrated biomass and moves toward the west coast of Florida driven by wind and the Loop Current, growth might be reduced or even stifled by strict controls on terrestrial runoff. To do this requires three major changes to present practice: 1) improved infrastructure for storm water management to cleanse, reduce or eliminate urban runoff, 2) replacement of septic systems in coastal watersheds and 3) significant reduction in nutrients released, from inland waters to the coast.

Each solution will take decades to implement, at considerable cost to counties, municipalities and the taxpayer. Since infrastructure in coastal communities lacks inventory as to age and condition, every county or municipality, within the boundaries of a coastal watershed, would have to conduct an audit of existing facilities as to their functionality, and then do a *pro forma* of improvements, to be ultimately paid for by the taxpayer. As an example, in 2012, the City of Naples amended its stormwater master plan to "require removal of the City's stormwater beach outfalls."[132] Draining three hundred ninety-five acres of highly urban development, the city expects to spend at least $70 million for improvements. A large part of the problem was created by smaller houses covering about 30% of a lot being torn down and replaced with large homes covering as much as 80% of a lot, with impervious materials, placing more pressure on stormwater drains to handle rainfall off roofs and pool decks that at an earlier time percolated into groundwater through lawns and pervious areas.

The second change, replacement of existing septic systems in coastal counties, was covered extensively in the previous chapter. It carries the same cost burdens as management of stormwater runoff.

Solutions—blue-green algae as a vexing problem

In the case of blue green algae coming down the Caloosahatchee and St. Lucie rivers, the first step would be to control the flow of terrestrial waste into Lake Okeechobee, from agricultural operations. Currently, approximately 81% of the phosphorous washing into the lake comes from north of the lake and Orlando to the Kissimmee Lakes area. Another 10% comes from the Everglades Agricultural Area (EAA), farmed heavily by the politically connected and federally subsidized sugar industry. Many EAA farms have largely stopped back pumping nutrients, but remain primarily responsible for legacy phosphorous, in the muck at the bottom of the lake.[133] Farms and ranches north of the lake are responsible for keeping their own animal waste confined to the edge of the farm, but this is based upon a voluntary commitment to Best Management Practices (BMPs). There is no regular inspection or verification of compliance.

The Florida Department of Environmental Protection target rate, in 1986, for phosphorous in Lake Okeechobee, is forty ppb vs the current average of about one hundred twenty ppb. To get to that lower number, loading into the lake should not exceed one hundred forty tons. Target unloading for the Everglades south of the lake is ten ppb. If the first target of one hundred forty tons is reached, marshes lining the littoral zone of the lake will eventually start to clean up the sediment. Estimates are it would take fifty years.[134]

However, this does not solve the problem of historic nutrients that have accumulated at the bottom of the lake. There are estimated to be over 50, 000 tons of legacy phosphorous poured in over the years and still accreting as muck covering 300 sq. miles of the lake's total area of 730 sq. miles.[135]

When algae cells die, they settle into the deepest parts of Lake Okeechobee. As they decompose, they begin to deplete oxygen. One solution, proposed by Paul Gray of Florida Audubon, is to manage the lake levels to reflect seasonality. During the wet season, lake levels would be allowed to rise giving the littoral zone plants the opportunity to consume nutrients in order to grow. During the dry season, those plants would decompose, reflecting the normal death and germination cycle of plant life, along the edges of the lake. Whether this would eventually reduce the muck level is open to question.

Another way to deal with the problem is by dredging. In a 2019 project called "Suck the Muck," Dane County, Wisconsin, is removing about 43,000 tons of sludge from the bottom of Dorn Creek. Cleaning up the thirty-three-mile long creek, with a build-up on the bottom of two to three feet, will take four years and about 1,500 truckloads. However, the creek is shallow enough to be able to move equipment along the bank to remove the sludge; Lake Okeechobee's muck is not nearly as accessible.

Allure of the quick fix

We need to be wary of the siren's song leading to the quick fix. Governor DeSantis, after a trade trip, began to tout a Tel Aviv company called Blue Green, for its algae killing technology. The company, after testing its product in Israel, did the first application in the United States at Chippewa Lake in Ohio, with notable success. The technology, in a product called Lake Guard, uses copper sulfide (CuS) spread as a powder on the surface of a waterbody. Using the diffusion power of wind and tide, the application is done in small doses but spreads quickly. The compound then sinks to the bottom where it interacts with organic matter in the sediment.

There is no good data on the effect of this product on the benthic habitat. The company remarks that an application "...[enables] living organisms the freedom to avoid direct contact by diving or simply moving upwind."[136] Glibly put and easy for a fish, but tougher for an oyster or clam. Given the failed experiments with copper sulfate (CuSo$_4$), in the Gulf of Mexico, in 1957, there is reason to be extremely cautious about using copper sulfide. The only difference between the two being that copper sulfate has an oxygen element in it, while copper sulfide does not. The unintended consequence of applying this kind of product to sensitive ecosystems needs careful long-term study, before being applied on a broad basis.

The multi-agency problem

A potential impediment to swift and effective decision-making is the multiplicity of state and federal agencies involved in overseeing the development, growth and movement of phytoplankton blooms. In Florida, there are five state and four federal departments responsible for various pieces of discovery, monitoring and public notification of the presence of harmful algal blooms. At the state level: FDEP, Department of Health, Fish and Wildlife Conservation Commission, Water Management Districts and county governments. From the federal side: EPA, U. S. Army Corps of Engineers, National Oceanic and Atmospheric Administration and United States Geological Survey.

Nowhere within the functions of government do more agencies interact than in the coastal regions where harmful algae blooms thrive.

An interesting confirmation of this problem was set forth in a lawsuit filed, in 2012, by an environmental group challenging FDEP and EPA. In its filing, the state responded to one of the petitioner's arguments this way: "There is more support for the record for the proposition that nutrient pollution in Florida is caused by a fragmented and uncoordinated regulatory systems than for Petitioners proposition that nutrient pollution is due to the Department's narrative criteria." [137]

In all fairness, today the tasks assigned to each agency are clearly identified and separated but require coordination. For example, the counties, water management districts are responsible for sampling and reconnaissance while FDEP and the Fish and Wildlife Conservation Commission carry the burden of analysis and dissemination of results. If the sampling results indicate a problem, the Department of Health and the counties are then responsible for advising the public. The back and forth between agencies works honed by time and experience, but it is cumbersome and sometimes time consuming.

Enforce existing regulations

As noted above, the FDEP set a target of one hundred forty tons for phosphorous loading into Lake Okeechobee, to be met by 2015. As of 2019, that goal had not been met. In 1986, the loading was four hundred twenty-one metric tons; in 2017, it was four hundred eighty-four metric tons.[138] While the sources of the problem are legion, they range from urban runoff from the fast-growing Orlando region, to dairy and cattle farms in the Kissimmee Lakes area, to farms in the Everglades Agricultural Area and to over management of the lake itself. A multiplicity of regulations exists which, were they enforced, would lead to an improvement in the situation, rather than a continuing downward spiral—as was the case, from 1986 to 2017.

Constant and reliable funding

Science is speculative, subject to review and revision. Too often, uncertainty becomes the veil for complacency and inaction, but science should guide the future direction of efforts to deal with harmful algae blooms. As consensus builds, it should be embraced and supported, with little regard to the political fallout. But that is naïve, for in the public sector, ongoing resources are needed for continuous monitoring, to give citizens adequate warning about the potential hazards and the presence of toxins in Florida's coastal waters. The mechanisms for detection and notification are in place and funding has not been a problem, given the spate of recent outbreaks. However, if blooms diminish in the future, it is likely that the commitment to finding solutions will follow the same path. That is the history of the last seventy years; it should not be in the future.

Much science in the past has been funded by independent grants, private foundations and non-profits like the Marine Biological Laboratory at Woods Hole. Given the political realities, and history, in Florida, sustained financial support of scientific efforts will continue to rely upon initiatives like the Red Tide Institute at Mote Marine, in partnership with the State of Florida, to offer hope to scientists that their work, and their future, will have sustained, ongoing and predictable funding.

Coordination

Lastly, there needs to be coordination among all scientific efforts, to study harmful algae blooms, from initiation to dissipation. This was the purpose in forming ECOHAB which has worked fairly well, in keeping lines of inquiry, supported by finite resources, unduplicated and in guiding government agencies and independent scientists toward research priorities. ECOHAB's goal, stated in simple terms is: "to develop and understanding of the population dynamics and trophic impacts of harmful algal species which can be used as a basis for minimizing their effects on the economy, public health, and marine ecosystems." [139]

No single reference site could adequately cover the biophysical aspects of harmful blooms, so ECOHAB serves as a repository of information, from peer-reviewed studies, collected from all over the world, to be publicly shared with investigators. ECOHAB needs to be given even broader authority to initiate studies into the origins, causes and effects of red tide and blue-green algal outbreaks.

There will always be research projects outside the mainstream like Paul Cox's work on BMAA and neurodegenerative diseases. That is nature of science which sometimes proves that assumptions and techniques once altered can lead to very different conclusions.

Final thoughts

Our future as a species depends upon a safe and available supply of fresh water. While over 70% of the planet is covered by water, only a little more than 2% is fresh, and less than half of that is easily accessible, with the rest being trapped in glaciers and snow at the polar extremes. One might argue that global warming will eventually melt the ice caps, but flowing in liquid form it will be quickly absorbed by and integrated into the world's oceans unless we find the means to trap and transport it to populated parts of the planet.

In a way, we are like Dorothy, trapped in a situation from which we can escape but choose not to. But the similarity breaks down in that we are caught in something we created. To break out of it will take time and money and a willingness to shed the mantle of comfortable complacency that allows us to believe the solution belongs to the next generation.

It does not. It belongs to us.

ENDNOTES

[1] The sex of a sea turtle is determined by temperature, which in turn depends to some extent upon the density of the sand. 82 degrees seems to be the tipping point between male and female. As the planet warms, it is likely that more females will be born.

[2] See Sneed Collard and Larry Ogren: "Dispersal Scenarios for Pelagic Post-Hatchling Sea Turtles," *Bulletin of Marine Science*, 47 (1): 233-243, 1990.

[3] Jeff Schmid, interview with the author, February 27, 2014.

[4] Jeff Schmid, e-mail to the author, March 3, 2014.

[5] Time on the surface is measured by the strength and duration of the transmitter signal.

[6] Jeff Schmid, interview with the author, February 27, 2014.

[7] Larry Brand and Angela Compton, "Long-term increase in *Karenia brevis* abundance along the Southwest Florida Coast," University of Miami, 2007.

[8] Cabeza de Vaca, Álvar Núñez. "The Journey of Álvar Núñez Cabeza de Vaca and his companions from Florida to the Pacific 1528-1536." Translation of La Relacion, ed. Ad. F. Bandelier. New York, Allerton Book Co. 1904

[9] Translated by Hugo Magana in Hugo a Magana, Cindy Contreras, Tracy A. Villareal: "A Historical Assessment of Karenia Brevis in the Western Gulf of Mexico." *Harmful Algae*, 2003.

[10] D.A.Nunez Ortega, "Esayo de Una Explicacion del origen de las grandes mortandades de peces en el Golfo de Mexico," *La Natutral* 6, 188-197, 1879.

[11] Ingersoll, Ernest: "On the Fish-Mortality in the Gulf of Mexico." Proceedings of the United States National Museum, 4, 1882, p. 74.

[12] *Ibid.,* p. 75.

[13] *Ibid.,* p. 76.

[14] *Ibid.,* p. 79.

[15] Porch, C.E., S.C. Turner, and M.J. Schirripa. 2007. "Reconstructing the commercial landings of red snapper in the Gulf of Mexico from 1872 to 1963." *Red snapper ecology and fisheries in the U.S. Gulf of Mexico,* editors W.F. Patterson, J.H. Cowan, G.R. Fitzhugh, and D.L.Nieland, American Fisheries Society Symposium 60, 337-353.

[16] Hoy, C., "Fish Mortality in the Gulf of Mexico." Proceedings of the U. S. National Museum 6, 1884, p. 107

[17] *Sunland Tribune,* Tampa, July 20, 1882

[18] Porter, Joseph Y., "On the Destruction of Fish by Poisonous Water in the Gulf of Mexico." *Proc. U. S. Nat. Mus.,* 4: 121.

[19] Glennon, A. H.: "Fish killed by poisonous water." *Bulletin of the U. S. Fish Commission,* 6, 1887. p 10.

[20] Report of the Commissioner: *Rep. U. S. Comm. Fish.* Part II, 1885, p. 69.

[21] Taylor, Harden F.: "Mortality of Fishes on the West Coast of Florida." Bureau of Fisheries Document 848, U.S. Government Printing Office, 1917.

[22] *Ibid.,* p. 7.

[23] *Ibid.,* p. 9

[24] *Ibid.,* p.13.

[25] *Ibid.,* p. 17.

[26] *Ibid.,* p. 19.

27 Galtsoff, Paul: "Progress Report on the Investigations of the Cause of the Mortality of Fish Along the West Coast of Florida Conducted by the U. S. Fish and Wildlife Service and Cooperating Organizations." *Special Scientific Report 46. (reissued)* Washington 1954

28 *Ibid.,* p.12.

29 *Ibid.,* p. 13.

30 LaPointe, Brian E., Laura W, Herren and Sara N. Ouly. Reducing Septic Tank Pollution in Charlotte County: Background Research Scope of Work, Florida Atlantic University – Harbor Branch Oceanographic Institute; Marine Ecosystem Health Program, 1988.

31 Staff report, The Florida Red Tide: Bureau of Commercial Fisheries Biological Laboratory, Fishery Leaflet 506, Galveston (undated).

32 Feinstein, Anita, A Russell Ceurvels, Robert F. Hutton and Edward Snook: Red Tide Outbreaks off the Florida West Coast. Marine Laboratory, University of Miami, March 1955. p. 23.

33 *Ibid.*

34 Odum, Howard T., J. B. Lackey, Jacqueline Hynes, Nelson Marshall: Some Red Tide Characteristics during 1952-1954, p. 25. *Bulletin of Marine Science of the Gulf and Caribbean,* vol. 5, no. 4, 1955. pp. 252-253.

35 *Ibid.,* p. 256.

36 Rounsefell, George A., and John E. Evans: Large-scale Experimental Test of Copper Sulfate as a Control for the Florida Red Tide. U. S. Fish and Wildlife Service, Special Report – Fisheries 270, Washington, D.C., December, 1958. p. 6.

37 Rounsefell, George A. and Walter F. Nelson: Red Tide Research Summarized to 1964 Including an Annotated Bibliography. Bureau of Commercial Fisheries, Special Scientific Report- Fisheries No. 535, 1964

[38] *Ibid.*, p. 17.

[39] Originally known as *gymnodinium brevis* in 1948, taxonomy syntax required a change to Ptychodiscus in 1979. Then, in 2000, the alga was rebranded as *Karenia brevis* in honor of Karen Steidinger, a long-time researcher on red tide most recently with the University of South Florida, Florida Institute of Oceanography.

[40] Smayda, T.J.: Harmful algal blooms: their ecophysiology and general relevance to phytoplankton bloom sin the sea. *Limnology and Oceanography,* 42 (1997).

[41] Fish and Wildlife Research Institute: Florida Fish and Wildlife Conservation Commission, 2006. http://www.floridamarine.org.

[42] With the acronym ECOHAB (Ecology and Oceanography of Harmful Algal Blooms), ECOHAB believed that unduplicated scientific inquiry would be desirable using researchers from throughout the country with specialized knowledge and equipment. First funded in 1998 and later reauthorized in 2004 and 2014, the program seeks competitive grant proposals from scientists throughout the United States to work toward a greater understanding of the origin, nature and effects of blooms along the country's coasts.

[43] ECOHAB: The Ecology and Oceanography of Harmful Algal Blooms – A National Research Agenda. http//:www.whoi.edu/science/B/redtide/nationplan/ECOHAB/ECHOHABExecSummary.html

[44] Magaña, Hugo A., and Tracy A. Villareal, The effect of environmental factors on the growth rate of Karenia brevis (Davis) G. Hansen and Moestrup. *Harmful Algae 5,* 2006. p. 192-198.

[45] The diel cycle is used by biologists to replace the diurnal cycle.

[46] Van Dolah, Frances M., Kristy B. Lidie, Emily A. Monroe, Debashish Bhattacharya, Lisa Campbell, Gregory J. Doucette, Daniel Kamykowski: The Florida red tide dinoflagellate Karenia brevis: New insights into cellular and molecular processes underlying bloom dynamics. *Harmful Algae,* p. 563.

[47] Evans, Terence J., Gary J. Kirkpatrick, David F. Millie and David J. Chapman: "Photophysical Responses of the Red-tide dinoflagellate *Gymnodinium breve* (Dinophyceae) under natural sunlight." *Abstracts from the Symposium on Harmful Marine Algae in the U.S.*, 2000.

[48] Del Castillo, Carlos E., Paula G. Noble, Robyn N. Conmy, Frank E. Muller-Karger, Lisa Vanderbloomen, Gabriel Vargo: "Multi Spectral In-Situ Measurements of Organic Matter and Chlorophyll Fluorescence in Seawater: Documenting the Intrusion of the Mississippi River Plume in the West Florida Shelf." Research Note Submitted to *Limnology and Oceanography*, December 2000.

[49] Tester, Patricia A. and Karen A. Steidinger: "Gymnodinium breve red tide blooms: Initiation, transport and consequences of surface circulation." *Limnology and Oceanography*, pp. 1039 – 1051, 1997.

[50] Maze, G, M. J. Olascoaga, L. Brand: "Historical analysis of environmental conditions during Florida Red Tide." *Harmful Algae*, 50, pp. 1 – 7, 2015.

[51] Walsh, John J. and Karen Steidinger: "Saharan dust and Florida red tides." *Journal of Geophysical Research*, Vol. 106, No. C6, pages 11,597 – 11612, 2001.

[52] Kubanek, Julia, Melissa K. Hicks, Jerome Naar and Tracy A. Villareal: "Does the red tide dinoflagellate Karenia brevis use allelopathy to outcompete other phytoplankton?" *Limnology and Oceanography*, 50(3), 2005, pp. 883-895.

[53] See https://mote.org/news/nutrients-that-feed-red-tide-under-the-microscope-in-major-study/

[54] The last six items listed in bold face came from the ECHOHAB project.

[55] Heisler, J., et al :hj "Eutrophication and Harmful Algal Blooms: A Scientific Consensus." *Harmful Algae*, December 2008, 1-13. See https://www.ncbi.nim.nih.gov/pmc/articles/PMC55343702/

[56] Rosen, B.H., Davis, T.W., Gobler, C.J., Kramer, B.J., and Loftin, K.A., 2017, "Cyanobacteria of the 2016 Lake Okeechobee Waterway Harmful Algal Bloom." U.S. Geological Survey Open-File Report 2017–1054, 34 p., https://doi.org/10.3133/ofr20171054.

[57] Secchi disc is a round dish with alternate black and white pie shaped cuts. Lowered in the water it measures turbidity and transparency.

[58] Carmichael, W. "A Status Report on Planktonic Cyanobacteria (Blue-Green Algae) and their Toxins." EPA/600/R-92/079, 1992.

[59] Paerl, Hans W., Timothy G. Otten and Raphael Kudela: "Mitigating the Expansion of Harmful Algal Blooms Across the Freshwater-to-Marine Continuum." *Environmental Science and Technology*, 2018, 52, 5519-5529, p. 5525.

[60] https://coastalscience.noaa.gov/news/study-explores-airborne-health-risks-from-cyanobacteria-blooms-in-florida/

[61] https://www.usgs.gov/news/usgs-finds-28-typescyanobacteria-florida-algal-bloom/

[62] https://myfwc.com/about/inside-fwc/fwri/

[63] Either directly detected or reported by reliable sources to Florida authorities.

[64] Anderson, Donald A., Sylvia Galloway, Jeanne Joseph: Woods Hole Oceanography Institute Tech. Rept., WHOI 93-02. p.1.

[65] Pierce, R. H. Mote Marine Red Tide Studies July 11, 1994 – June 30, 1995, submitted to Florida Department of Environmental Protection as Technical Report No. 429. 1995.

[66] The West Indian manatee was listed as "endangered" under the Endangered Species Act until 2017 when the estimated count of the fast recovering population was 8,810 and the animals were down listed to "threatened."

[67] https://www.mmc.gov/priority-topics/species-of-concern/florida-manatee/

[68] Interview with the author February 9, 2019.

[69] https://www.whoi.edu/science/B/redirect/nationplan/ECOHAB/2. ECOHABProgram.html, p.1.

[70] Restudy Plan Report, Governor's Commission for a Sustainable South Florida, January 20, 1999. p. 42.

[71] *Ibid.*, p.41.

[72] Comments made at a panel discussion February 6, 2019.

[73] 2018 Florida Rev. Statutes, 379.2271.

[74] *Tampa Bay Times*, August 8, 2018.

[75] Hu, Chuanmin, Frank E. Muller-Karger and Peter W. Swarzenski." Hurricanes, submarine groundwater discharge, and Florida's red tides." American Geophysical Union, 2006.

[76] Heil, Cynthia A., Marta Revilla, Patricia M. Gilbert and Sue Murasko: "Nutrient quality drives differential phytoplankton community composition on the southwest Florida Shelf." *Limnology and Oceanography*, 52(3), p. 1074.

[77] Brand, Larry and Angela Compton: "Long-term increase in *Karenia brevis* abundance along the Southwest Florida Coast." *Harmful Algae*, 2007, p. 232.

[78] *Ibid.*, p.242.

[79] *Ibid.*, p. 239

[80] Alcock, Frank: "An Assessment of Florida Red Tide: Causes, Consequences and Management Strategies." Mote Marine Technical Report #1190, August 2007, p. 2.

[81] *Ibid.*, p. 1.

[82] The federal agencies named were: National Oceanographic & Atmospheric Administration, Environmental Protection Agency, U. S . Geological Survey, U. S. Fish and Wildlife Service, Federal Emergency Management Agency; state agencies were: Department of Environmental Protection, Department of Community Affairs (eliminated in 2012), Florida Fish and Wildlife Conservation Commission, Department of Health, Public Service Commission; local and regional agencies were: Regional Planning Councils, Water Management Districts, Local city and county governments, Special Surface Water Management Districts, and local Water Authorities.

[83] The five areas were: prediction, freshwater blooms, salt water blooms, scientific assessment of hypoxia and methods of reducing bloom impacts (RDDTT plan)

[84] Jewett, E.B., Lopez, C.B., Dortch, Q., Etheridge, S.M., Backer, L.C.: "Harmful Algal Bloom Management and Response: Assessment and Plan," Interagency Working Group on Harmful Algal Blooms, Hypoxia, and Human Health of the Joint Subcommittee on Ocean Science and Technology,Washington, D.C., August 2008.

[85] *Ibid.,* p. 15.

[86] *Ibid.,* p.11.

[87] *Ibid.,* p 12.

[88] *Ibid.,* p. 15.

[89] Taylor, Harden F., "Mortality of Fishes on the West Coast of Florida." Bureau of Fisheries Document No. 848. Washington D.C., U. S. Government Printing Office, 1917, p. 6.

[90] *Ibid.,* p. 7.

[91] Rounsefell, *ibid.*

[92] *Ibid.*

[93] Watanabe, Takashi, Richard Lockey and Joseph Krzanowski, Jr.: "Airway Smooth Muscle Contraction Induced by *Ptychodiscus Brevis* (Red Tide) Toxin as Related to a Trigger Mechanism of Bronchial Asthma." *Immunology and Allergy Practice,* May 1988.

[94] Thomas J. O'Shea Galen B. Rathbun Robert K. Bonde Claus D. Buergelt Daniel K. Odell: "An Epizootic of Florida Manatees Associated with a dinoflagellate bloom." *Marine Mammal Science*: April 1991 https://doi.org/10.1111/j.1748-7692.1991.

[95] Dong-Ha Nam, Douglas H.Adams, Leanne J. Flewelling, Niladri Basu: "Neurochemical alterations in lemon shark (*Negaprion brevirostris*) brains in association with brevetoxin exposure." *Aquatic Toxicolofy,* September 2010. https://doi.org/10.1016/j.aquatox.2010.05.014

[96] Li, Zongchao et al: "Risk in daily newspaper coverage of red tide looms in Southwest Florida." *Applied Enviromental Educational Communications,* 2015: 14 (3).

[97] *Ibid.*

[98] https://www.newscientist.com/article/12217747"

[99] https://www.ncbi.nlm.nih.gov/pubmed/18461767.

[100] Rosen, B.H. et al.: "Understanding the effect of salinity tolerance on cyanobacteria associated with harmful algae blooms in Lake Okeechobee, Florida." U. S. Geological Survey Scientific Investigation Report 2018 -5092.

[101] Zanchett, Giliane and Eduardo C. Oliveira-Filho.: "Cyanobacteria and Cyanotoxins: From Impcts on Aquatic Ecosystems and Human Health to Anticarcinogenic Effects." *Toxins* 2013. Pp. 1896-1917.

[102] *Ibid,* p. 1905.

[103] EPA: Drinking Water Health Advisory for Cyanobacterial Microscystin Toxins.

[104] https://www.ncbi.nlm.nih.gov/pubmed/29791446

[105] Banack, S.A., Murch, S.J. and Cox, P.A., 2006. Neurotoxic flying foxes as dietary items for the Chamorro people, Marianas Islands. *Journal of ethnopharmacology, 106*(1), pp.97-104.

[106] Dunlop, R.A., Cox, P.A., Banack, S.A. and Rodgers, K.J., 2013. The non-protein amino acid BMAA is misincorporated into human proteins in place of L-serine causing protein misfolding and aggregation. *PloS one,* 8(9), p.e75376.

[107] Rodgers, K.J. and R. Dunlop: "The cyanobacteria-derived neurotoxin BMAA can be incorporated into cell proteins and could thus be an environmental trigger for ALS and other neurological diseases associated with misfolding [abstract]." Presented at 22nd Annual Symposium on ALS/MND, Sydney, Australia, December 1, 2011.

[108] Ueno, Y., Nagata, S., Tsutsumi, T., Hasegawa, A., Watanabe, M.F., Park, H.D., Chen, G.C., Chen, G. and Yu, S.Z., 1996. Detection of microcystins, a blue-green algal hepatotoxin, in drinking water sampled in Haimen and Fusui, endemic areas of primary liver cancer in China, by highly sensitive immunoassay.

[109] Myhre, Oddvar *et al.*: "Repeated five-day administration of L-BMAA, microcystin-LR, or as mixture, in adult C57BL/6 mice—lack of adverse cognitive effects." *Sci Rep.*8, 2308 (2018).

[110] Cox, P.A., Davis, D.A., Mash, D.C., Metcalf, J.S. and Banack, S.A., 2016. Dietary exposure to an environmental toxin triggers neurofibrillary tangles and amyloid deposits in the brain. *Proceedings of the Royal Society B: Biological Sciences,* 283(1823), p.20152397.

[111] Karamyan, V.T. and Speth, R.C., 2008. Animal models of BMAA neurotoxicity: a critical review. Life sciences, 82(5-6), pp.233-246.

[112] N. Chernoff, D. J. Hill, D. L. Diggs, B. D. Faison, B. M. Francis, J. R Lang, M. M. Larue, T.-T. Le, K. A. Loftin, J. N. Lugo, J. E. Schmid & W. M. Winnik: "A critical review of the postulated role of the non-essential amino acid, β-N-methylamino-L-alanine, in neurodegenerative disease in humans," *Journal of Toxicology and Environmental Health,* Part B, 20:4, 183-229, DOI: 2017 10.1080/10937404.2017.1297592

113 Davis, David et al: "Cyanobacterial neurotoxin BMAA and brain pathology in stranded dolphins." PloS ONE 14(3) e0213346. https://doi.ord/10.1371/journalpone.0213346. (2019).

114 There is scientific evidence that stingrays and sharks use magnetic fields to navigate.

115 Rush, T. X Liou and D. Lobner: "Synergistic toxicity of the environmental neurotoxins methylmercury and Beta-N-methylamino-L-alanine." Neuroreport 23, 216-219, 2012.

116 Falkowski PG, Katz ME, Knoll AH, Quigg A, Raven JA, Schofield O, Taylor FJR: The Evolution of Modern Eukaryotic Phytoplankton. *Science.* 2004, 305: p. 354-360.

117 O'Neil, J.M., T.W. Davis, M.A. Buford and C.J. Gobler: "The rise of harmful cyanobacteria blooms: The potential roles of eutrophication and climate change." *Harmful Algae*, February 2012 pp. 313-334.

118 Olexa, Michael, Tatiana Borisova and Jarrett Davis: Handbook of Florida Water Regulation: Florida Air and Water Pollution Control Act. University of Florida IFAS Extension 2017.

119 https://ballotpedia.org/Environmental policy in Florida

120 Letter to Governor Lawton Chiles, October 1, 1995.

121 *Ibid.*

122 Florida Administrative Code: Rule 62-302.530 (47) (b)

123 Florida Administrative Code, Rule 62-302.400

124 Florida Department of Environmental Protection, *Integrated Water Quality Assessment for Florida, 2008.*

125 Florida Department of Environmental Protection, *Final Integrated Water Quality Assessment for Florida.* 2018.

126 https://myfloridalegal.com/ago.nsf/Opinions/9083F168C353A7218 52563F600673D09

127 SB 216 and HB 141

[128] SB 214 and HB 85

[129] SB 1322 and HB 343

[130] SB 1278 and HB 405

[131] *Fort Myers News-Press*, July 1, 2019.

[132] See https://www.naplesgov.com/streetsstormwater/page/beach-outfalls

[133] For more information see https://http://www.evergladeshub.com/okeechobee/okeechobee.htm

[134] Katrine Elsken, *Lake Okeechobee News*, December 2018.

[135] Gray, P.N., C. J. Farrell, M. L. Krause, A. H. Gromnicki, eds. Audubon of Florida: Lake Okeechobee: A Synthesis of Information and Recommendations for its Restoration, 2005

[136] Company brochure, Lake Guard Blue: A Novel Algicide, Designed to Effectively Treat Harmful Algal Blooms in Waterbodies.

[137] State of Florida, Division of Administrative Hearings Case No. 11-6137RP

[138] Elsken, Karen: Muck on lake bottom complicates phosphorous loading problem. *Lake Okeechobee News*, January 7, 2018.

[139] https://www.whoi.edu/science/B/redtide/nationplan/ECOHAB/ECOHABExecSummary. html